W9-AAH-987

779.5
STE

DATE DUE

DEMCO, INC. 38-2931

Oregon

OREGON BY ROAD

Celebrate the States

Oregon

Rebecca Stefoff

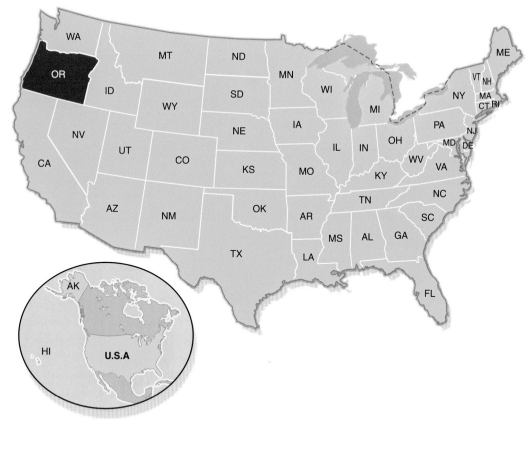

mc Marshall Cavendish
Benchmark
New York

Marshall Cavendish Benchmark
99 White Plains Road
Tarrytown, NY 10591-9001
www.marshallcavendish.us

All Internet sites were correct and accurate at time of printing.

Library of Congress Cataloging-in-Publication Data

Stefoff, Rebecca, 1951–
Oregon / by Rebecca Stefoff.—2nd ed.
p. cm. — (Celebrate the states)
Summary: "Provides comprehensive information on the geography, history, governmental structure,
economy, cultural diversity, and landmarks of Oregon."—Provided by publisher.
Includes bibliographical references and index.
ISBN 0-7614-2022-3
Oregon—Juvenile literature. I. Title. II. Series.
F876.3.S735 2006   979.5—dc22   2005015949

Editor: Christine Florie
Editorial Director: Michelle Bisson
Art Director: Anahid Hamparian
Series Designer: Adam Mietlowski

Photo research by Candlepants Incorporated

Cover Photo: Philip James Corwin/Corbis

The photographs in this book are used by permission and through the courtesy of; *Corbis:* Steve Terrill,
8, 22, 69; Craig Tuttle, 10, 105; Galen Rowell, 11, 35; Charlie Munsey, 13; Gary Braasch, 15, 83;
Wolfgang Kaehler, 17, 103; Corbis, 19, 32, 36, 45, 46, 48, 49, 129; Paul Edmondson, 20; Philip James
Corwin, 28, back cover; James L. Amos, 29; Dave G. Houser, 30; Darrell Gulin, 54, 117(lower), 125;
Shepard Sherbell, 57; Bohemian Nomad Picturemakers, 59; Warren Morgan, 61, 66, 95; Charles
O'Rear, 62; Catherine Karnow, 65, 102; Owaki-Kulla, 71, 100; Richard Cummins, 76; Kevin R. Morris,
86, 112; Lawrence Manning, 89; George D. Lepp, 90; Bill Stormont, 92; Michael Boys, 93; Phil
Schermeister, 94, 109, 128; Joel W. Rogers, 98; Owen Franken, 107; Tom Bean, 113; Buddy Mays, 115;
David Aubrey 117(lower); Ian Rose, 121; Mark Savage, 131; Roger Ressmeyer, 133; Kevin Schager,
136. *The Image Works:* A. Vossberg, 21. *Minden Pictures:* Yva Momatiuk/John Eastcott, 23; Jim Branden-
burg, 24. *Photo Researchers Inc.:* Lawrence E. Naylor, 25. *Animals/Animals:* Lon Lauber, 26. *Oregon
Historical Society:* 33, 38. *Getty Images:* 39, 43. *Pacific University Archives:* 41. *AP Wide World Photos:*
Don Ryan, 72, 78; Rick Bowmer, 80. *SuperStock:* Richard Cummins, 74; David W. Middleton, 84.

Printed in China
1 3 5 6 4 2

Contents

Oregon Is . . .

To Native Americans and pioneers, Oregon was a paradise.

"Many Chinooks still believe that the Creator placed them—along with the mountains, valleys, the life-giving rivers, and all the plants and animals—in this region at the beginning of time."

> —Chief Cliff Snider, Chinook Tribe, Portland, Oregon, 2003

"[Father] told us about the great Pacific Ocean, the Columbia River and beautiful Willamette Valley, the great forests and the snowcapped mountains. He then explained the hardships and dangers, the suffering and the dreary long days we would journey on and on before we would reach Oregon."

> —Martha Gay, who came to Oregon from Missouri at age fourteen in 1851

"Here we are at last in Oregon City . . . that long looked-for place!"

> —settler Esther Hanna, 1852

Today people still follow their dreams west.

"I wanted nothing more than to live in that most charmed of places . . . that Oregon."

> —Sallie Tisdale, Oregon writer

"I'd heard about the wild horses out here, and horses always drew me to them."

> —John Sharp of Prineville, age eighty-nine, on why he came to Oregon from Oklahoma at age seventeen

"The skate parks are way better here. Also, I can finally learn to surf."

> —Eric Croy, age fifteen, who moved with his family to Portland, Oregon, from Minnesota in 2004

Oregon's history reaches far into the past . . .

"The [Columbia] river Indians had been one of the world's most stable, prosperous societies. Families passed their culture from generation to generation, an unbroken chain that stretched through millennia."
— *The Oregonian*, December 7, 2003

"Today, Jacksonville's future lies in her past. Part of the business district looks much as it did at the turn of the century. The citizens of Jacksonville have preserved their past by restoring many historic buildings."
—Chamber of Commerce, Jacksonville, National Historic Landmark District

. . . while Oregonians struggle to shape the state's future and define its identity.

"More than half a million people are expected to move here by the year 2010. Let's be ready for them."
—Vera Katz, mayor of Portland, 1995

"Not the Old West, not the New West, but the Real West."
—suggested new state slogan from Steve Corey, Pendleton, 2003

KEEP OREGON WEIRD.
—bumper sticker seen in Portland and Eugene, 2004

Oregon has a little of everything. Within its borders are mountains, gentle valleys, caves, old-growth forests, wild rivers, glorious beaches, and deserts. Native Americans, white and black Americans, and immigrants from Asia and Latin America meet and mingle here. Farms and orchards share the landscape with fast-growing cities and high-technology industries, but wilderness remains close at hand. Oregonians believe that everyone else secretly wants to be in Oregon. Maybe they're right.

Chapter One

A Beautiful Landscape

Nestled between the states of California and Washington, bordered on the north by the mighty Columbia River, Oregon is part of the Pacific Northwest. When people think of the Pacific Northwest, they often picture a rainy, tree-covered landscape. Oregon is like that in places, but it is much more. The diversity of Oregon's people and ways of life is mirrored in the great variety of its landscapes.

English traveler William Broughton was one of the first Europeans to explore Oregon and to describe it for the rest of the world. After Broughton spent three weeks on the Columbia River in 1792, he called Oregon "the most beautiful landscape that can be imagined." Broughton saw Oregon's lush forests, meadows filled with flowers and berries, and abundant wildlife. However, this green and fertile garden was only the living surface of the land. Beneath it lay the bones of the earth, formed in fire and flood.

Oregon's diverse landscape is one of rugged coastlines, green forests, rolling hills, colorful meadows, deserts, lava beds, and lofty mountains.

VOLCANOES AND RIVERS

For millions of years the eastern part of Oregon and Washington seethed and bubbled. From time to time lava burst from volcanoes or from huge cracks in the earth to flow like fiery mud over thousands of square miles of territory. The lava cooled and hardened into the high, flat plateau that is central and eastern Oregon.

Later, around 12 or 13 million years ago, the earth pushed up a new range of volcanic mountains in western Oregon. These mountains, called the Cascades, run through the state from south to north. Some of them are still active volcanoes. In Portland, Oregon's largest city, people sometimes see smoke or steam rising from the top of nearby Mount Hood.

Eight thousand years ago—just yesterday, in Earth's long history—one of the peaks in the southern Oregon Cascades blew its top. "That explosion must have been the loudest noise ever produced in this part of the world," said an Oregon volcanologist. Water filled the huge, empty crater and became Crater Lake, which is almost six miles wide and close to two thousand feet deep. In 1980 a volcanic explosion in Mount Saint Helens, just over the border in Washington, filled the sky north of Oregon with an immense cloud of ash. Earthquakes and lava flows in the volcano in early 2005

The vivid red, pink, bronze, tan, and black rock layers of the Painted Hills in the John Day Fossil Beds are a result of weathered volcanic ash.

Crater Lake holds approximately 4.6 trillion gallons of water and is the seventh deepest lake in the world at 1,932 feet.

led some Oregonians to wonder if their northern neighbor would soon blow up again.

The Pacific Northwest is frequently shaken by earthquakes, which often occur around volcanoes. In 1993 a quake rattled Portland and was felt for hundreds of miles as a reminder of the earth's awesome power. The center of the quake was thirty miles south of Portland. Earthquake expert Ian Madin warned Portlanders, "There's no particular reason to believe that the next one isn't going to be closer to home."

Other earthquakes have rattled Oregon in recent years, including one in 2002 that was centered near Mount Hood. Scientists measured it at 4.5 magnitude—a medium-sized quake. It did little harm, but if it had occurred under Portland or another densely settled area, the outcome might have been different. In 2000 scientists discovered that an earthquake fault line runs beneath Portland's West Hills. This raised concerns that a major earthquake could severely damage the city.

To the north, Mount Saint Helens showed new signs of life in late 2004 and early 2005, with minor quakes and plumes of steam and ash that hinted at the possibility of another volcanic outburst. Oregon's volcano watchers also turned their attention to the group of Central Oregon peaks called the Three Sisters, where swarms of small earthquakes revealed that volcanic activity might be on the rise. Some experts think that one of the volcanoes, South Sister, could produce Oregon's next eruption.

Water as well as fire has helped shape Oregon. The largest river in the state is the Columbia, which flows south from Canada and then turns west to the Pacific Ocean. Over many centuries this powerful river carved its channel through layer upon layer of rock, so that it now flows to the sea through the Columbia Gorge, a narrow passage between high, sheer cliffs. The gorge forms the border between Washington and Oregon.

Hells Canyon is another river gorge, located on Oregon's eastern border with Idaho. Here the Snake River winds through a rugged canyon that is eight thousand feet deep in places—several thousand feet deeper than the Grand Canyon. After riding a raft through the rapids of the Snake River, travel writer Richard Lovett called Hells Canyon "one of the least-known but most spectacular places in North America."

The Oneonta Gorge, part of the Columbia Gorge, is so narrow that in places, the Oneonta Creek fills the narrow passage from wall to wall.

Rivers have cut smaller canyons into Oregon's high central plateau. The Deschutes and John Day rivers flow into the Columbia. In western Oregon, the Rogue and the Umpqua race from the Cascades down to the sea.

The Willamette River also runs through western Oregon, but it does not empty into the sea. Instead it flows north through a wide valley to meet the Columbia. Although most of Oregon's rivers are filled with rapids and waterfalls that make them difficult to navigate, the Willamette is broad and flat. The early settlers used it as a "highway" for travel in western Oregon.

Sometimes, though, the rivers turn deadly. In February 1996 unusually warm temperatures melted snow in the mountains of western Oregon. Snowmelt poured downhill and mixed with heavy rains. Twenty-six rivers flooded. As the rivers kept rising, volunteers and National Guard crews worked around the clock to pile sandbags along Portland's Willamette River and in front of shops and homes in dozens of towns. A woman who skipped work to help a sandbag crew in Milwaukie said, "I got to the point of saying my community is more important than my job."

The floods left seven Oregonians dead, one missing, and forty-six injured. More than 22,000 people had to leave their homes. Most returned to mud-soaked floors and ruined furniture. "The things you lose . . . aren't your carpet or your sofa," a woman in the small town of Mist said sadly. "It's when you open up that cedar chest and there are the letters from your kids, destroyed by water and mud."

The Cascade Range is Oregon's defining geographic feature. It cuts the state in two, although roads through a number of passes link the western and eastern parts together. People who live west of the Cascades are called wetsiders, while those who live to the east are called drysiders.

The 240-mile Willamette River flows through one of the country's most fertile regions.

LAND AND WATER

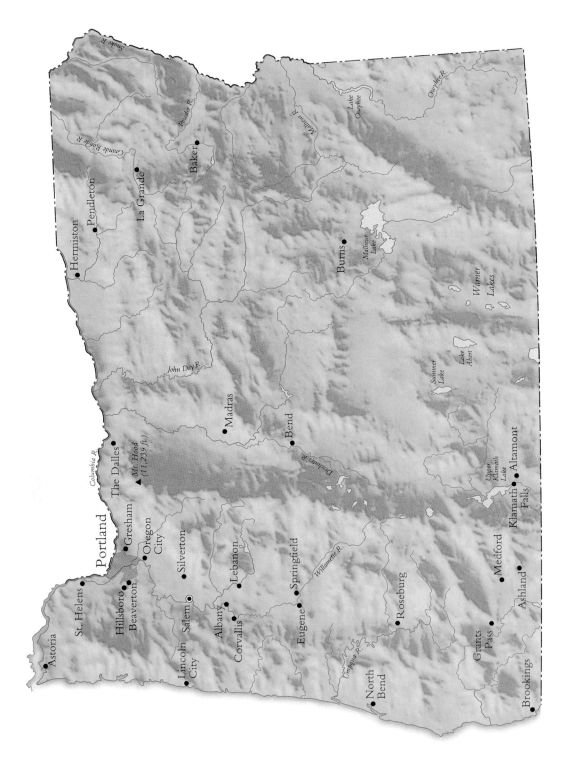

Snake R.

Powder R.

Grande Ronde R.

Pendleton

Hermiston

La Grande

Baker

Malheur R.

Lake Owyhee

Owyhee R.

Burns

Malheur Lake

Warner Lakes

John Day R.

Lake Abert

Summer Lake

Madras

Bend

Columbia R.

The Dalles

Mt. Hood (11,239 ft.)

Deschutes R.

Upper Klamath Lake

Altamont

Klamath Falls

Portland

Gresham

Oregon City

Silverton

Medford

St. Helens

Hillsboro

Beaverton

Salem

Albany

Lebanon

Springfield

Willamette R.

Roseburg

Ashland

Grants Pass

Brookings

Astoria

Lincoln City

Corvallis

Eugene

Umpqua R.

North Bend

THE WET WEST

The western third of Oregon is the land of trees, moss, and rain. The area between the Pacific Ocean and the Cascade Range gets between 20 and 130 inches of precipitation each year, with rainfall heaviest at the coast. In the mountains much of this precipitation falls as snow. Elsewhere it comes as rain—the soft, steady drizzle called Oregon mist.

Between October and May it can rain almost every day. The constant gray gloom gets on some people's nerves. William Clark, one of the first Americans to explore Oregon, certainly noticed it. On December 26, 1805, he noted in his journal, "Rain all day as usual." In several other places he mentioned that all of the members of the exploring expedition were "wet and miserable" from the rain. A few decades later, a pioneer girl

An umbrella can be quite handy along the coast, one of Oregon's wettest regions.

said, "My most vivid recollection of that first winter in Oregon is of the weeping skies and of Mother and me also weeping." Residents have learned to live with the rain. "Like many Oregonians," says resident Catherine Windus, "I often shun raincoat and umbrella during heavy showers, preferring to pretend it's not happening."

On the good side, the steady rainfall nourishes western Oregon's forests of huge cedar and fir trees and makes the region a fertile farming area. Western Oregon has a long growing season. Temperatures are generally mild. Along the Willamette, for example, winter temperatures rarely reach the freezing point, and summers usually bring no more than a dozen or so 90-degree Fahrenheit days.

Western Oregon is a geography sandwich: a valley between two mountain ranges. The long, narrow valley—called Willamette in the north and Umpqua in the south—is nestled between the Coast and Cascades ranges. The Coast Range runs along the edge of the Pacific Ocean. The Coasts are low, rounded mountains, wrapped in fog and heavily forested with spruce, cedar, and fir. In southern Oregon the Coast Range merges with a knot of taller, craggier peaks: the Siskiyou and Klamath ranges, which sprawl across the Oregon-California border. Oregon writer Sallie Tisdale calls the Klamath and Siskiyou region "a bleak, lonesome, extraordinarily beautiful place—beautiful the way the Moon is beautiful, or a comet come to Earth, or the spatter of stones across a beach."

The center of western Oregon's "sandwich" is the valley, flat and fertile in the north but hilly in the south as it begins to rise toward the mountains. East of the valley is another chain of mountains: the long line of the Cascades, separating west from east. At approximately 11,235 feet, Mount Hood in this range is Oregon's highest peak. The central and southern Cascades are dotted with lava fields and lakes.

Large amounts of precipitation over the Cascades have produced a region of dense forest.

The western slopes of the Cascades receive plenty of moisture, carried inland from the sea. They are covered with tall forests of Douglas fir, hemlock, cedar, and spruce and are carpeted with mosses and ferns. The high peaks keep rain-carrying clouds from traveling eastward, however, and the mountains' eastern slopes have drier, more open forests of ponderosa pine.

Oregon's western border is its Pacific Ocean coast. Although Oregon has some long, sandy beaches, much of the coastline consists of steep, rugged cliffs that drop to the wave-tossed waters, with only small pockets of beach between the capes and the headlands. Offshore, large rocks—some of them

The constant pounding of the surf upon Oregon's sea cliffs eroded them over time, creating the dramatic haystack rocks found off many of Oregon's beaches.

many times the size of a house—jut up from the whitecapped waves. Over the centuries, the waves have carved these rocks into pinnacles, arches, and cone-shaped forms called haystacks.

The beaches have signs warning of the hazards of Oregon's chilly ocean waters. Two of the major hazards are "sneaker waves"—big swells that appear unexpectedly and can submerge an unsuspecting beachgoer—and floating logs, which can be dangerous when tossed in the surf. Still, walkers, surfers, and swimmers flock to the coast, which offers abundant recreation as well as magnificent scenery.

THE DRY EAST

The eastern two-thirds of Oregon is a high desert plateau with mountains around the edges. The plateau receives eleven to seventeen inches of rain and thirteen to eighty-five inches of snow each year. Summers are hotter than those on the west side of the mountains, and winters are sunnier but colder. Temperatures as high as 119 degrees Fahrenheit and as low as –54 degrees have been recorded in eastern Oregon.

Oregon's large dry side contains several geographic regions. The middle of the state, from the eastern slopes of the Cascade Range to the headwaters of the John Day River, is known as Central Oregon. In this region, the open

Though mostly dry and sparse, Eastern Oregon makes up more than half of the state. Wildflowers bloom here during spring and summer.

pine forests of the mountains gradually give way to a plateau landscape of reddish-brown rock, sparsely covered with silvery green juniper and wild sage shrubs. In the spring and summer, though, the plain blazes with wildflowers: purple-blue lupins, orange-red Indian paintbrush, and hot pink fireweed.

At several places in Central Oregon, rivers and streams have carved deep canyons into the plateau. The Deschutes River and the Crooked River flow through such canyons. Throughout the region, clifftops and mesas are crowned with weathered, block-shaped rock formations that look like the ruins of ancient forts or castles. Made of a type of volcanic rock called basalt, they are relics of the long-ago era when lava flows covered the area.

In the center of the state is the Ochoco National Forest, a huge expanse of woodland that sprawls across several ranges of rolling hills. Broken by a few stretches of prairie, the forest extends into the low but rugged Blue Mountains of eastern Oregon. To the north, in the northeastern corner of the state, are the Wallowa Mountains near Hells Canyon. The Wallowas, with their steep, snowcapped granite peaks and alpine meadows and lakes, are sometimes called Oregon's Switzerland.

Southeastern Oregon is part of the Great Basin, the vast arid region that covers most of Nevada and parts of Utah, California, and the states of the Southwest. This part of Oregon

Eagle Cap Mountain is reflected in Moccasin Lake in the heart of the Wallowa Mountains.

is extremely dry. Its largest bodies of water are Harney and Malheur lakes. In the wettest years, Malheur Lake covers 125 square miles, but in dry years it shrinks until nothing is left but mud holes.

The southeastern corner of the state is a jumble of small mountain ranges: the Mahogany, Trout Creek, Sheepshead, and Pueblo. The area's tallest peak, 9,670-foot Steens Mountain, is a long ridge that rises steeply from the Alvord Desert, where tumbleweeds whirl across sands glistening white with salt. "Expect extreme hot, extreme cold, and oversized mosquitoes, but what country!" said Portlander Sandra Dorr after visiting Steens Mountain.

OREGON WILD AND TAMED

For centuries salmon have returned from the sea each year to lay their eggs in Oregon's rivers. Trout also live in the state's rivers and streams. Zane Grey (1872–1939), the famous author of many tales of Western adventure, was a fisherman who called the Rogue River "the best trout stream in the world." The rivers are also home to otters, beavers, and many kinds of waterbirds. Kingfishers, ospreys, ibises, sandhill cranes, blue herons, and eagles nest near Oregon's waterways or rest there during their yearly migrations.

Black bears were once common in many parts of Oregon. Today they are seldom seen

The beaver is Oregon's state animal. Beavers can be found along Oregon's coastal rivers and streams.

except in the wooded south. Elk still graze in open meadows at the edges of forests across the state, and mule deer and pronghorn antelope live east of the mountains. Cougars prowl remote areas. At night the eastern canyons echo with the yipping of coyotes. These wild relatives of the dog appear as gray-brown shadows in fields and even in suburbs all over the state.

Some of Oregon's most urgent conservation issues revolve around its endangered or threatened animals (thirty-six species) and plants (fourteen species). One species that has both worried and excited Oregonians is the gray wolf. Once common in Oregon, wolves were wiped out in the twentieth century because of fears they would kill ranchers' livestock.

Many environmental scientists later realized that wolves play an important role as predators in the Western ecosystem. In the early twenty-first century, wolves were reintroduced to the Rocky Mountain states. A few of them ventured from Idaho into eastern Oregon. A poll cited in a 2004 Sierra Club report showed that 70 percent of Oregonians wanted to let wolves return to the state, but many ranchers disagreed. In 2004, Sierra Club spokesman Patrick Shannon agreed that the state must find ways to protect ranchers from the loss of income if wolves kill their livestock. "Most importantly," Shannon added, "as the wolf returns to its historic range in Oregon, we need to make sure the first

Roosevelt elk, sometimes called Olympic elk, make their home along the coastal forests of Oregon.

actions we take are not to trap and kill it." The Oregon Department of Fish and Wildlife will decide how wolves will be treated in the state.

Wolves' future in Oregon remains uncertain, but one endangered species may be on the rise. The Western snowy plover is a small seabird that nests on ocean beaches. As human activity on beaches increased, nests were disturbed and the number of plovers

In an attempt to protect the breeding grounds of the Western snowy plover, beach restrictions have been enforced in Oregon.

fell. Attacks on eggs and baby birds by cats, crows, and other predators also helped place the plovers on the endangered-species list.

State wildlife officials acted to preserve the plovers by poisoning predators and providing better protection for nesting areas. Although some Oregonians have complained about new limits on beach areas during nesting season, the program is working. In 2004, 120 plovers nested on Oregon's coast. They reared 107 young birds, up from 60 the year before.

Oregon's most famous wild creature probably does not even exist. According to Native American legends and modern tales, the mountain forests are home to the Sasquatch, or Bigfoot, which resembles both a human and an ape. In 1971 a high-school music teacher named Rich Brown claimed he saw a Bigfoot near The Dalles, a city on the Columbia River. Brown raised his rifle but, as he said, "I couldn't shoot it because it looked more human than animal." There is no reliable evidence, however, that the Sasquatch is real.

WHOO'S FORESTS?

At 1.5 feet tall, with dark eyes and soft brown feathers dotted with white, the spotted owl doesn't look like a troublemaker. Since the late 1980s, however, the spotted owl has caused countless arguments throughout the Pacific Northwest.

Spotted owls live in the Northwest's old-growth forests, areas that have never been logged. Each pair of owls needs one thousand acres or more of forest to survive. Spotted owls cannot live in clearcuts, sections of forest in which all trees are cut down, or in the young forests that begin growing after an area has been logged. The owls are vanishing as old-growth forests are cut for timber. Scientists believe that only a thousand or so pairs remain.

The spotted owl has become a symbol of the conflict over the Northwest's remaining ancient forests. Environmentalists claim that the forests must be preserved because they are the habitat of a threatened species protected by law. Timber-industry representatives and loggers claim the environmentalists are "tree-huggers" who are only using the owls as an excuse to ban logging in old-growth forests.

A wildlife specialist with the National Audubon Society said, "Each is terribly important in its own right, both the owl and the forest. Time is running out to save both." Meanwhile, a forest worker in the timber town of Idanha drives a pickup truck with a bumper sticker that reads LOGGERS ARE AN ENDANGERED SPECIES. Both sides have turned to the federal government for support. Lawmakers must try to answer the question: how can we protect the owls and the forests and still continue to harvest the trees we need?

Sasquatches may be invisible, but humans have left their mark on the land. Native Americans used Oregon's resources to serve their needs, sometimes altering the landscape in the process. Groups who lived along rivers constructed nets and large wooden traps in the waterways to catch fish. Those who lived in the forested coastal region felled trees to build their large wooden houses and canoes. Native peoples also set fire to woodlands regularly in order to remove undergrowth and to provide places for berries and other foods to grow. They also cleared pathways through forests, built permanent settlements, and left painted and carved images on rock walls. The influence of Native Americans on the landscape, however, was minor compared to the changes made by those who came later.

The Willamette Valley, with its mild climate and fertile soil, was the target destination of the first white settlers. The valley remains Oregon's heartland, home to the majority of Oregonians. Today it is a row of cities strung along a ribbon of interstate highway. At the top of the row, where the Willamette River meets the Columbia, stands Portland, Oregon's largest city. One-third of Oregonians live in or near Portland.

Oregon's largest monuments to human activity are the four huge dams that span the Columbia River. The Bonneville Dam in the Columbia Gorge was completed in 1937. The Dalles Dam, the John Day Dam, and the McNary Dam followed in the 1960s.

These dams have changed the Northwest in many ways. They make it easier for barges to carry agricultural goods from Oregon's central plains to ports for shipping around the world. They provide water to irrigate the dry eastern fields. Most importantly, they produce hydroelectric power. During the second half of the twentieth century, the cheap electricity of the Northwest made the region attractive to industries that use a lot of power, such as metalworking and papermaking. The dams have allowed power companies

A National Historic Landmark, the Bonneville Dam was one of the largest hydroelectric projects of its time. Its uses include navigation, flood control, and energy resources.

in the Pacific Northwest to make so much electricity that they can sell the excess to Los Angeles and other cities.

At the same time, the dams have turned one of the most majestic wild rivers in the American West into a series of sludgy lakes. They have blocked the migration of salmon, which also have been hurt by pollution and soil runoff from logging operations. At one time, salmon hatched in the Columbia River in uncountable numbers. Today their population is dwindling fast.

The Native Americans of Oregon's Columbia River region have a stake in the survival of salmon, which for centuries served as a major food source for many tribes. Natives have gone to court to defend the fishing rights granted to them by treaties, and they also have launched programs to protect the salmon. The Confederated Tribes of the Umatilla Indian Reservation, for example, have restored salmon to the Umatilla River and are working to develop a fish-recovery plan based on both Western science and native culture.

Everywhere in Oregon, people are changing the land. Ranchers graze thousands of head of cattle on the eastern grasslands, many of which are owned by the federal government. Environmentalists point out that cattle pollute streams and destroy whole ecosystems, but ranchers believe that the land should be used to support families and communities.

A similar problem appears in fast-growing Portland. As people move into the area, they need places to live, work, and shop. Developers want to cut down trees and build houses and malls on some of the parkland in which Portlanders take such pride. At the heart of the debate is the Urban Growth Boundary (UGB), created in 1980 to define the urban land available for residential and industrial development in the city—to prevent malls and housing developments from spreading into farmland in a process called urban sprawl. Population growth has led to many changes in the UGB over the years. In 2002, for example, the city government enlarged the UGB to enclose nearly 20,000 additional acres. This inspired fears that urban sprawl is unavoidable. The struggle is sure to continue between those who want to protect what is left of wild Oregon and those who want to complete its taming.

Native American tribe members fish for salmon using large nets. The Native Americans in Oregon have taken great steps toward restoring the region's salmon runs.

Chapter Two

Yesterday and Today

The first Oregonians were the ancestors of today's Native Americans. They came to Oregon ten thousand years ago, maybe earlier, as part of a great migration that carried people from Siberia and northern Asia into Alaska and North America. They settled first on the eastern and central plateau, then along the Columbia River, and finally on the coast.

NATIVE AMERICAN BACKGROUND

Gradually the settlers formed almost a hundred different bands and tribes, speaking more than thirty distinct languages. Each group developed a culture shaped by its environment and the available resources. These Native American groups fell into three broad categories: the Coast and Western peoples, the Columbia Plateau peoples, and the Great Basin peoples.

The Coast and Western groups lived along the Pacific Ocean coast, in the Coast Mountains, in the valleys west of the Cascade Range, and on the western slopes of the Cascades. Their environments were heavily forested, with much rainfall and generally mild temperatures. The cultures of these Indians resembled those of other native peoples who lived in similar conditions from northern California all the way to southeastern Alaska.

The Whispering Giant Totem honors coastal Oregon's native tribes.

The Chinook lived in longhouses that could hold dozens of people. They were constructed of wood and were between twenty to seventy feet long.

Among the native groups in western Oregon were the Chinookans of the lower Columbia River and the Tututni and Chetco of the southern coast. The Coquille, Coos, Lower Umpqua, Suislaw, Alsea, and Tillamook Indians lived along the rivers that run into the coast. The Tualatin, Santiam, Yoncalla, and others inhabited the northern valley, while in the southern valley lived the Upper Umpqua, Cow Creek, Shasta, and Takelma peoples.

All of these native groups ate diets based on fish, berries, and game. They lived in houses of cedar and used canoes for hunting sea life. Those who lived along the shore gathered shellfish, while those in the valleys added acorns and nutritious roots to their diets. Their highly developed crafts ranged from carved cedar canoes along the Columbia River mouth to ornate baskets of woven grass and razor-sharp blades chipped from volcanic rock in the south.

In the interior of the state, east of the Cascades, lived the peoples of the Columbia Plateau, including the Wasco, Wishram, Tenino, Cayuse, Umatilla, and Nez Percé groups. In a region of cold winters and hot summers, they tended to migrate with the seasons. They spent the summer months in high camps in the mountains, where game and berries were plentiful, and the winter months at lower sites along the rivers, where they caught and dried fish to eat and to trade with other tribes. The summer dwellings of these Plateau people were airy and cool—pole frames covered with mats of woven grass. In winter, they sought warmth in pit houses that were sunk into the earth and covered with thick roofs of sod and brush.

In a painting by J. E. Stuart that was made around 1884, Native Americans establish a fishing camp along the Columbia River.

The Great Basin peoples lived in the southern part of the state, a challenging landscape of rock and sparse water supplies that often gave out during hot, dry weather. Here the Klamath, Modoc, Bannock, Northern Paiute, and Western Shoshone peoples developed a way of life that moved with the seasons over wider areas than those covered by the Plateau Indians. In family groups or small bands, many of them traveled two hundred miles or more each year, from their winter homes on lakeshores to their summer and autumn hunting grounds high in the mountains. Water birds, deer, antelope, and rabbits were their principal game. They also gathered berries, roots, seeds, and nuts, often leaving food in hiding places called caches to provide nourishment on future journeys.

EXPLORERS AND MISSIONARIES

The name *Oregon* is probably an Indian word, but no one knows its source. By the 1760s people in Europe and America were using it as the name of a big river that was thought to flow through the West. Gradually the term *Oregon country* came to mean all of the Northwest, including what is now the province of British Columbia in Canada.

Explorers first came to Oregon looking for a waterway called the Northwest Passage. They hoped the passage would become a trade route linking eastern North America with the Pacific Ocean. The explorers never found this Northwest Passage, because it does not exist. However, they did explore Oregon, first by water and later by land.

Spanish and British sailors began exploring the Oregon coast in the sixteenth century. The first white American to set foot on the coast of Oregon was Robert Gray, a New England sea captain, who landed there in 1788. Four years later, on another voyage, Gray came upon the Columbia River, which he named after his ship.

THE COYOTE GOD

Tommy Thompson was a chief of the Wy-am people along the Columbia River (above). Before he died in 1959 at about a hundred years old, Thompson passed on the Wy-am legends to younger members of the tribe. Many legends tell of Spilyay, or Coyote. Spilyay was a wise, clever, mischievous god, sometimes called the Trickster. He played tricks on other animals and on people, but he helped them, too. Coyote appears in legends not only of the Wy-am people, but also of many other Native American groups.

According to Wy-am legend, in the time before men and women lived on the earth, the salmon could not leave the ocean. Coyote was a giant, and very powerful. He dug a long, deep trench east from the ocean so that the salmon could swim upstream to have their young. That is how the Columbia River came to be.

Coyote is known as the Changer because his great trench changed the world. After the salmon could swim upstream, the earth was ready to be a home for men and women. The first people appeared in the world during this Changing Time.

"Ocean in view! Oh! the joy!" wrote William Clark in his journal on November 7, 1805. No wonder Clark was overjoyed to see the Pacific. Together with his companions—Meriwether Lewis; forty or so other men, including Clark's black slave, York; and a Shoshone woman named Sacajawea—Clark had been traveling toward the ocean for eighteen months, all the way from St. Louis, Missouri.

Army officers Lewis and Clark traveled to Oregon at the request of President Thomas Jefferson. In 1803 the United States had bought a huge tract of land from France. Called the Louisiana Purchase, it stretched from the Mississippi River to the Rocky Mountains. Jefferson had long been curious about these western lands, and as soon as the Louisiana Purchase was complete, he sent the Lewis and Clark expedition out to explore them.

Sacajawea of the Shoshone people accompanied Lewis and Clark across the unchartered Western wilderness.

Jefferson gave the expedition several tasks. One was to explore the West—above all, to locate a water route from the Mississippi River to the Pacific Ocean, if one existed. Another task was to gather information about the plants, animals, peoples, and resources of the West. Lewis and Clark were also expected to establish trade relations with the Native American groups they met. Jefferson wanted these groups to knew that the U.S. government now claimed the lands of the Louisiana Purchase.

Lewis and Clark and their party were the first known Americans to cross the continent to its western coast. After spending the winter of 1805–1806 at a fort they built on the Oregon coast, they made their way back east. Their journey succeeded in part because of the considerable help they received from Indians who provided them with shelter, food, and guides along the way. Upon their return they presented Jefferson with dozens of sample plants and animals, as well as new information about the tribes, climate, and geography of the West. When reports of the expedition were published, along with William Clark's map of its route, many Americans felt a keen desire to follow in the explorers' footsteps and to see for themselves the remarkable regions Lewis and Clark had visited.

Meriwether Lewis was particularly enthusiastic about the Willamette Valley. He called it "the only desirable situation for a settlement which I have seen on the West side of the Rocky Mountains." Lewis believed the valley could hold as many as 50,000 Americans. He would be amazed to see almost 2 million people living there now.

The Lewis and Clark expedition excited Americans about Oregon. The Oregon country was not yet part of the United States, however. Both the United States and Great Britain claimed the land. In 1818 the two nations agreed to share the territory, opening the way for American settlement in Oregon.

Valley of the Willamette River *by Henry Warre (1845) depicts a landscape suitable for settlement.*

THE OREGON TRAIL

Explorers, fur trappers and traders, missionaries, and settlers began trickling into the Willamette Valley in the 1820s. Many of them were helped by Dr. John McLoughlin, a Canadian official of Britain's great Hudson's Bay Company. McLoughlin was based in present-day Washington State, but because he was generous to the American settlers in the Willamette Valley he is remembered as one of Oregon's founders.

The first missionary to arrive in Oregon was Jason Lee, a Methodist who hoped to convert the Indians of the Willamette Valley to Christianity. He established a mission near present-day Salem in 1834. Other

Protestant missionaries soon followed. The first Roman Catholic priest arrived in Oregon country in 1838. By founding schools and churches, the missionaries encouraged settlement.

In the 1840s the trickle of settlers became a flood. Thousands of people traveled westward on a wagon-train route that came to be called the Oregon Trail. The trail ran for almost two thousand miles from Independence, Missouri, to Oregon City, just south of present-day Portland. A branch of the trail went south to California.

It was the lure of free land that drew the settlers west to Oregon. Between 1840 and 1870, 250,000 people crossed the continent on the

By 1900 almost half a million people had traveled west on the Oregon Trail to establish farms in the Willamette River Valley or to seek their fortune in gold in California.

Oregon Trail. Most of them traveled with their families, and many were children. Historian Lillian Schlissel called their journey "one of the great migrations of modern times."

"We were a happy carefree lot of young people, and the dangers and hardships found no resting place on our shoulders," said Susan Parrish, who took the Oregon Trail at age seventeen. The journey brought great hardship, however. Nearly every wagon train lost one or more people to disease, accident, starvation, or Indian attack—and many Native Americans, too, were killed by the travelers.

The hardest part of the trip came at the end, in Oregon. Travelers were low on food and supplies. They were weary after months on the road, and so were the oxen that pulled their battered wagons. After the travelers dragged their wagons up one side of the steep Blue Mountains with ropes or chains, then lowered them slowly down the other side, they faced a difficult choice: should they make the risky voyage by raft down the raging Columbia to the Willamette Valley, or should they try the brutal route across Mount Hood? "Today climbed a mountain that broke my animals' hearts. Near broke mine too," one pioneer who took the land route wrote in his journal.

By mountain or river, settlers reached Oregon and began building communities. As these communities grew, so did the feeling that Oregon ought to be part of the United States.

STATEHOOD

American settlers in Oregon begged the federal government in Washington, D.C., to establish firm control over the Oregon country. One of them, a former fur trapper named Joe Meek, rode all the way to the nation's capital to make the request.

THE MOTHER OF OREGON

Tabitha Brown (below) was sixty-six years old when she left Missouri to start out on the Oregon Trail in 1846. She wasn't looking for adventure. Brown joined the wagon train because two of her children were taking their families to Oregon and she did not want to be parted from them.

Brown's journey was not an easy one. A wagon overturned. A little girl died of scarlet fever, and a little boy fell under wagon wheels and was crushed. Then things got worse. In Idaho, Brown and a number of others from her wagon train decided to try a shortcut to the Willamette Valley, but their route led them into the Nevada desert and the Klamath wilderness. "Our sufferings from that time," Brown wrote later, "no tongue can tell."

Brown was tough. Some of the travelers died, but she made it through to the Willamette Valley. She had lost everything but one small coin. Brown used that coin to buy needles and went to work making gloves. Eventually she made enough money to help build one of the oldest schools in the West, today's Pacific University. The Oregon legislature named Tabitha Brown the Mother of Oregon in 1987.

In 1846 the United States and Britain divided the Oregon country. Britain got the northern part, which is now British Columbia, a province of Canada. Congress named the southern part the United States Oregon Territory and asked Abraham Lincoln to be its first governor. He turned down the job, so Congress sent General Joseph Lane instead.

By the 1850s the territory was growing fast. Asa Lovejoy and Francis Pettygrove founded a new town at the meeting place of the Columbia and the Willamette rivers. They flipped a coin to see who would get to name the new town. Pettygrove won. He was from Maine, so he loyally named the town after the city of Portland, Maine.

Portland quickly became an important port and center of trade. Unlike some settlements in the Wild West, Portland was said to be orderly and respectable. An early historian of the city wrote, "Affairs of blood are not common; house breaking, violent robbery, or affrays are but few. Public tumult is unknown."

In 1853 the government designated the northern half of Oregon as the Washington Territory. On March 15, 1859, the ship *Brother Jonathan* sailed into Portland Harbor with the news that Oregon had become the nation's thirty-third state. After being moved several times from its original location in Oregon City, the state capital was established in Salem.

Oregon's progress into statehood was not entirely peaceful. As early as 1847, George Abernethy, the settlers' elected leader, had warned of trouble with the Native Americans. "They see the white man occupying their lands, rapidly filling up the country, and they put in a claim for pay," Abernethy said. "They have been told that a chief would come out from the United States and trade with them for their lands; they have been told this so often that they begin to doubt the truth of it."

The influx of East Coast pioneers and merchants increased Oregon's population, leading to the creation of the Oregon Territory in 1848 and statehood a decade later.

TREATIES AND RESERVATIONS

Congress made the Oregon country into an official territory in 1848. One of the first acts of the new territorial government, working together with Congress, was to transfer ownership of the best land in the territory away from the Native American inhabitants and to make it available to the incoming whites.

Treaties and reservations were the tools the government used to take control of Indian lands. Congress authorized commissioners in the Oregon Territory to make treaties with Native American leaders. According to Congress, the commissioners' goal was "to leave the whole of the most desirable portion [of the land] open to white settlers."

In 1850 Congress went further, passing the Oregon Donation Land Law, which allowed white settlers to claim millions of acres formerly occupied by Oregon's Coast and Western tribes. The result was violence, often bloody and fatal, between natives who wanted to remain in their traditional homelands and whites who wanted to drive them out. The government's solution was to move the Indians to reservations, which were established on tracts of land far from white settlement. Most of them were unsuitable for farming and had limited resources.

The native peoples of the Willamette, Umpqua, and Rogue valleys were forced onto the Siletz and Grande Ronde reservations near the coast. Unable to hunt and gather food in their traditional territories, the Indians suffered greatly from hunger. Like Native Americans everywhere, they also suffered greatly from diseases transmitted by whites. Illnesses such as smallpox and measles, to which Native Americans had never been exposed before the arrival of Europeans, wiped out massive numbers of Indians—far more than perished in battle.

Some of Oregon's Indians left the reservations to seek work as laborers on white-owned farms or in businesses (above right). Partly because of these departures, but mostly because of high death rates on the reservations, the number of Indians enrolled at Siletz dropped from 2,026 in

1856 to 438 in 1900. Other reservations experienced similar losses. As Chief John of the Rogue River people declared to the government of Oregon after his people had been relocated to a reservation, "It is not your war but your peace that has killed my people."

The history of treaties with the native peoples of Oregon is a history of broken promises. In 1931, at a land-claims hearing on the Warm Springs Reservation in Central Oregon, a long-lived member of the Tenino tribe remembered some of those promises. Albert Kuckup was about one hundred years old at the time. He reported that in 1855, when he was a young man, he had attended the Wasco Council, a treaty negotiation between the government and several of the Plateau tribes that led to the founding of the Warm Springs Reservation.

At the Wasco Council, the Plateau tribes asked that the reservation be created along the Columbia River so that they could continue to fish in their traditional way. Joel Palmer, Oregon's superintendent of Indian affairs, replied that that was impossible. He claimed that it was necessary for the Indians' safety to remove them from the river, along which many white people would be traveling. Palmer did promise the Indians that they would be able to use the forests, fish, animals, and berries on their reservation, and they would be able to pass to and from the Columbia for fishing. That promise was soon broken, however, when whites took control of the forests and tried to prevent the Indians from fishing and hunting. Recalling the long-ago treaty council and Palmer's empty promises, Kuckup told the hearing, "The government didn't tell me when you make treaty you take the forestry, you take the game and you take the fish, berries, and roots within."

Trouble broke out in 1847 in the Cayuse War, the first of a series of Indian wars in the Northwest. As the whites forced Indians off their traditional homelands, some Indians fought back. Wars broke out in the Rogue River area in the 1850s and in central and eastern Oregon in the 1860s and 1870s.

One man who became a symbol of the Native American struggle was In-mut-too-yah-lat-lat, born in the Wallowa Valley around 1840. His name means "Thunder Traveling to Loftier Mountain Heights." Whites knew him as Chief Joseph.

Chief Joseph became a leader of the Nez Percé people. In 1877, after gold was found in Nez Percé

Chief Joseph was best known for resisting the U.S. government's attempts to force his tribe onto reservations. He died in 1904.

territory, the U.S. government ordered Joseph and his people to move to Idaho. After a fight in which three Nez Percé killed some settlers, Joseph tried to escape with his people to Canada. Men, women, and children traveled for 1,600 miles through the mountains into Montana, with the army in pursuit. At last, footsore, cold, and starving, the Nez Percé surrendered. They were taken to Indian territory in Oklahoma, where half of them fell sick and died. Chief Joseph ended his days on a reservation in Washington. He was never allowed to return to the Wallowa Valley.

POPULATION GROWTH: 1850–2000

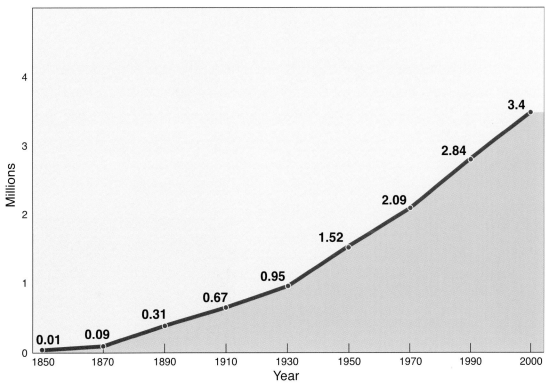

MODERN OREGON

Oregon's population and economy boomed after railroads reached the state in the 1880s. Portland grew fast, from 90,000 people in 1900 to 200,000 just ten years later.

Eastern Oregon's growth was based on gold, grass, and grain. Gold strikes lured prospectors to the state's interior in the 1860s, grass offered grazing for huge herds of cattle and sheep, and grain farmers in the northeast part of the state soon made wheat one of Oregon's leading exports.

Logging exports grew, too. By 1900 Oregon was the nation's third-largest producer of timber. Many of the fighter planes in World War I (1914–1918) were built of Oregon wood.

Portland was bursting with boosterism during the opening years of the twentieth century. Boosterism refers to the way that civic and business leaders energetically talked and wrote about their community's advantages and bright future—they "boosted" Portland, hoping to attract still more residents, businesses, and investments. Portland's newspaper, the *Oregonian*, boasted that Portland's population outnumbered Seattle's by ten thousand people in 1900. William Wells, editor of the Portland magazine *Pacific Monthly*, claimed, "There is no place in the world where the optimist has more chance of realizing his greatest dreams."

The centerpiece of all this boosterism was a grand fair held in Portland in the summer of 1905 to celebrate the one-hundredth anniversary of Lewis and Clark's arrival on the Pacific coast. The Lewis and Clark Centennial and American Pacific Exposition and Oriental Fair, as the organizers called it, was the first world's fair to take place on North America's West Coast. Its purpose was to show the world that Portland was no longer a rough frontier town. Instead, it was a cultured metropolis with business ties to Asia and the rest of the world.

The Lewis and Clark Exposition not only honored the explorers who paved the way to the West Coast, it also highlighted the commerce, technology, and resources of the region. This is the Forestry Building from the 1905 Exposition.

With conferences on health, education, and city government, a large amusement arcade, and exhibits from sixteen states and twenty-one foreign countries, the fair attracted 1.6 million visitors. More than 400,000 of them were from outside the Pacific Northwest. As they entered the fairground on the bank of the Willamette River, all visitors passed under the motto WEST-WARD THE COURSE OF EMPIRE TAKES ITS WAY—a proud declaration of Portland's identity as the end result of the decades-long exploration and settling of the American West.

The Great Depression of the 1930s brought economic hardship throughout the United States, and Oregon was no exception. In 1934 Governor Julius Meier said, "Oregon is dead broke." Yet the Depression left a lasting legacy to Oregonians. The Civilian Conservation Corps (CCC) was a federal program that helped the jobless by giving them work on public lands. In the state's national forests, CCC crews built roads, hiking trails, and bridges that are still used today.

The economic picture brightened when the United States entered World War II in 1941 and Oregon became a center of shipbuilding. War industries provided 160,000 jobs, attracting workers from other states. After the war, when soldiers returned to the United States and bought houses, America's timber industry boomed. Oregon became the nation's leading timber producer in 1950.

Oregon shipbuilders lay the keel of the USS Liberty, *a freighter built in the early 1940s.*

ROLL ON, COLUMBIA

A series of huge dams were built along the Columbia River in the late 1930s. Folksinger Woody Guthrie remembers the invitation in 1940 to "come up to the Columbia River to the Bonneville and Grand Coulee dams . . . to walk up and down the rivers, and to see what I could find out to make up songs about. I made up twenty-six." This is the most beautiful.

Green doug-las fir where the wa-ter cuts through, Down the wild

can-yons and val-leys she flew, Pa - ci - fic North - west to the

o - cean so blue, It's roll on, Co - lum-bia, roll on.

Chorus

Roll on, Co - lum - bia, roll on,

Roll on, Co - lum - bia, roll on, Your

pow - er is turn - ing the dark - ness to dawn, It's

roll on, Co - lum - bia, roll on.

Other great rivers add power to you,
Yakima, Snake, and the Kickitat, too,
Sandy, Willamette, and Hood River, too;
Roll on, Columbia, roll on! *Chorus*

Tom Jefferson's vision would not let him rest,
An empire he saw in the Pacific Northwest.
Sent Lewis and Clark and they did the rest;
Roll on, Columbia, roll on! *Chorus*

At Bonneville now there are ships in the locks,
The waters have risen and cleared all the rocks,
Shiploads of plenty will steam past the docks,
So, roll on, Columbia, roll on! *Chorus*

And on up the river at Grand Coulee dam,
The mightiest thing ever built by a man,
To run to great factories for old Uncle Sam;
It's roll on, Columbia, roll on! *Chorus*

For decades Oregon was a well-kept secret. Oregonians were deeply attached to their state, but the rest of the country didn't pay much attention to it. The editors of *Oregon Times* magazine wrote that during the 1950s and 1960s, "We existed largely as rumor, trudging along in a remote rainbelt and forever a little . . . out of it." Then, in 1975, a research organization announced that Portland was the most livable city in the country. Portland journalist David Sarasohn, only half joking, calls that announcement "the greatest natural disaster ever to strike Oregon."

Year after year the Pacific Northwest's reputation for livability grew. The populations of Portland and of Seattle, Washington, soared as people from other parts of the country moved to the Northwest. They loved the region's natural beauty, good schools, low prices and crime rate, and mild weather. Before long, old-time residents grumbled that the Northwest was becoming trendy.

INTO THE TWENTY-FIRST CENTURY

The rush of people to the Northwest has undermined what brought them there in the first place. Prices and crime have risen, and rapid population growth has put more pressure on the environment. The major development in Oregon's history at the dawn of the twenty-first century was not an event. Instead, it was a growing understanding of the significant differences among various parts of the state.

By the end of 2003, Oregon was home to 3.5 million people. The state has become a very diverse collection of regions, each with its own distinctive character, ways of life, and economic opportunities and challenges. These regions often disagree about goals and values. Urban Oregonians who support protection for old-growth forests, for example, are at odds with rural people whose towns and economies are tied to the logging industry.

The *Oregonian*, the state's largest newspaper, highlighted the strong differences within Oregon in a series of articles about "The Nine States of Oregon." The articles showcased the features of regions such as Central Oregon, with an emphasis on recreation and the state's fastest-growing population; the coast, home to many retired people; Cowboy Country in the southeast, the biggest region with the smallest population; and Portlandia, the zone that includes the state's largest city, whose residents pay more than half of the state's total income taxes.

Governor Ted Kulongoski, who faced the challenge of bringing the regions together to solve statewide questions, called the map of Oregon a "tapestry" of differing ideas and needs. "I'm trying to figure out what is the common thread that runs through these communities," he said.

With a reputation for doing things its own way, Oregon made the news for clashing with the federal government on several issues in the 2000s. One is physician-assisted suicide, which the voters of Oregon approved in the Right to Die Law, despite the opposition of the U.S. Justice Department. Another is medical marijuana, which physicians in Oregon can prescribe to patients to control pain.

Debates and differences of opinion are a way of life in Oregon, and that's not likely to change. The state's population is expected to keep growing rapidly. Oregonians face the challenge of preserving what they love about their state for future generations to cherish. Science-fiction writer Kate Wilhelm, who moved from Florida to Oregon, once said that Oregon's future is safe—as long as Oregonians continue to value their children and their trees.

Chapter Three
Living in Oregon

Oregon's population is changing and becoming more diverse. The 2003 census showed that just over 88 percent of Oregonians were white and non-Hispanic, down from more than 90 percent a decade earlier. The state's population was 9 percent Hispanic American; 3 percent Asian, Hawaiian, and Pacific Islander; 3 percent mixed race; 2 percent African-American; and 1 percent Native American. The fastest-growing group in the population is Hispanic American, and the majority of that group are people of Mexican descent.

ETHNIC OREGON

White people were a minority in early Oregon. In 1850 there were about 12,000 people in Oregon, including only 800 whites and 54 blacks. Most of the rest were Native Americans. A few Chinese immigrants had come north from California to work in the goldfields of southern Oregon.

People of Scandinavian, English, Irish, Scottish, German, Polish, and Italian ancestry came to Oregon in large numbers in the late nineteenth

Through festivals, rodeos, and other events, Oregonians celebrate their state's Western heritage and its ethnic diversity.

and early twentieth centuries. Swiss immigrants started the cheese industry in Tillamook. Finns settled at Astoria and elsewhere on the coast and helped establish the fishing industry.

Many Chinese immigrants came to Oregon in the 1870s and 1880s to work on building the railroads. After 1882, however, U.S. laws prevented Chinese people from coming to the United States, and Oregon's Chinese population stopped growing.

The laws that halted Chinese immigration grew out of a movement called nativism that arose in the United States in the mid-nineteenth century. Nativists opposed immigration, especially by immigrants who were non-white or non-Protestant. Although people of every race and religion had been present in North America since colonial times, nativists felt that the United States was and should remain a white, Protestant, Anglo-Saxon country. Their fears about immigration were based partly on racial or cultural prejudice and partly on the fear that immigrants, who were often willing to work at difficult jobs for low pay, would take work away from "real" Americans.

Fear and prejudice led to outbreaks of violence against immigrants. Oregon saw some violence against Chinese immigrants, as did other areas of the West, where newcomers from Asia were concentrated. Still, immigrants from Asia continued to come to the American West to seek opportunities not available to them in their homelands. When Chinese immigration was halted, Japan supplied the next wave of immigrants, many of whom contributed greatly to Oregon's economic development.

Some histories record that the first Japanese immigrant to Oregon arrived in 1860 and worked lighting gas lamps in Portland. A large number of Japanese men and women arrived in the 1880s to work on the railroads. Many of them stayed and became successful fruit growers in the Hood River Valley near Mount Hood.

Asian immigrants endured many hardships during the late 1800s. Today, however, Asian Americans in Oregon contribute to the economy of the state and offer diversity through their art, festivals, and foods.

Like Japanese Americans all over the western United States, Oregon's people of Japanese ancestry were forced into special camps by the army during World War II, when the United States went to war with Japan. Many lost their houses and land. Afterward some Japanese decided not to try to rebuild their former lives. Others came back to Oregon, however, and reestablished the state's Japanese-American community. Linda Tamura, a Japanese-American writer who grew up in Oregon, praises the strength of the men and women from Japan who survived "racial persecution, language barriers, strenuous labor, and financial hardships, while still maintaining their dignity and a loyalty for their new homeland."

ETHNIC OREGON

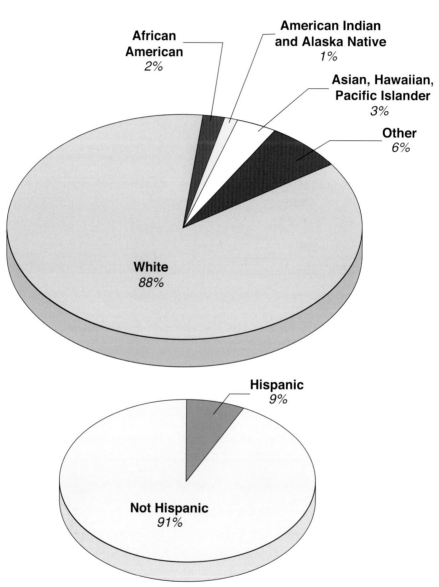

African American
2%

American Indian and Alaska Native
1%

Asian, Hawaiian, Pacific Islander
3%

Other
6%

White
88%

Hispanic
9%

Not Hispanic
91%

Note: A person of Cuban, Mexican, Puerto Rican, South or Central American, or other Spanish culture or origin, regardless of race is defined as Hispanic.

Native Oregon

Once there were as many as several hundred different groups or tribes of Native Americans in Oregon. Many of the smaller groups died out or merged with other tribes during the years of white settlement. Then, during the 1950s, the U.S. government ended its official recognition of another sixty-two tribes. In recent years half a dozen of these groups have successfully fought to have their tribal status restored.

Today Oregon has nine federally recognized tribes: the Burns Paiute Tribe; the Klamath Tribe; the Coquille Tribe; the Confederated Tribes of Grand Ronde; the Confederated Tribes of Siletz; the Confederated Tribes of Warm Springs; the Confederated Tribes of Umatilla Indian Reservation; the Confederated Coos, Suislaw, and Lower Umpqua Indians; and the Cow

Native Americans celebrate their cultural heritage at the Pendleton Round-Up.

Creek Band of Umpqua Indians. Fewer than half of the state's approximately 450,000 Native Americans, however, are enrolled as members of these tribes. Some of the Indians living in Oregon belong to tribes in other states. Others have no official tribal membership.

Almost 90 percent of Oregon's Indians live in cities. The rest live in rural settings, either on or off the reservations. Oregon's reservations differ greatly in size and ecology. Siletz, in the damp, forested coastal area, is the smallest reservation at 4,204 acres. Warm Springs, in the high desert country east of Mount Hood, is the largest, covering more than 644,000 acres. Each of the two reservations is home to about 3,600 people.

New Arrivals

African Americans had been coming to Oregon from the early days of exploration—one of the men who came west with Lewis and Clark was Clark's black slave York. The Oregon Territory, and later the state of Oregon, had "black" laws that prevented African Americans from settling there. By the early twentieth century, the laws were no longer enforced—but they remained on the books, a reminder of racial injustice, until the late 1920s.

In the early years of the twentieth century, Portland's African-American population was large enough to support several churches and a sprinkling of black-owned businesses. At first, blacks in Portland lived near the downtown train station because many of them worked for the railway companies or for downtown hotels. By law, African Americans could not own property downtown. After a new bridge built in 1913 connected the outlying district of North Portland to downtown, however, many black families moved to the neighborhood of North Portland in Albina, where they could buy homes. That neighborhood, with several historic African-American churches, is still the home of many of Portland's black residents.

During the state's early years, African Americans contributed to Oregon's growth through various occupations such as farmworkers, artisans, merchants, servants, skilled laborers, sailors, railroad workers, porters, waiters, cooks, and barbers. Today, African Americans make up 2 percent of the total population.

World War II (1941–1945) caused a significant increase in Oregon's African-American population. As many as 160,000 people came to the state to work in such war industries as shipbuilding and aluminum manufacturing, and about 10 percent of these newcomers were black. After the war, many of them remained in Oregon.

The most recent wave of Asian immigrants came to the United States to escape the Vietnam War and other wars in Southeast Asia. Between 1975 and 1993, 24,000 men, women, and children from Vietnam, Cambodia, and Laos settled in Oregon. They are working to forget old ethnic rivalries and to help one another. Says Paul Kinh Duong, "We quickly realized that we need to be together and support each other."

Many Southeast Asians have opened small restaurants or groceries in Portland. "Anybody work hard, they can succeed," says Pham Thu Trong, from Vietnam, who owns a small beef-noodle-soup restaurant. Life in America has brought new challenges, however. One is the rise of Asian-American youth gangs that prey on other Asians. Because of the gangs, jeweler Nguyen Truc keeps steel bars over the window of his store. "Even in Vietnam, in wartime, we didn't have to do this," he says. "There might be too much freedom here."

Oregon's Hispanic population rose during the 1940s and 1950s, when many Mexicans—most of them experienced agricultural workers—came to the United States under a policy known as the Bracero Program. The *braceros*, as the workers were called, came to the United States not as permanent settlers but as temporary farm labor. Still, the arrival of more than 350,000 Hispanics each year, mostly in the western states, strengthened the Hispanic presence and culture in Oregon and other parts of the country.

The Bracero Program ended in 1964, but people from Mexico and other Latin American nations continued to move north to work. For years they have found work in Oregon during the summer and fall, picking fruit, working on tree farms, and performing other seasonal agricultural tasks. Now many of them are staying, becoming part of Oregon's largest and fastest-growing minority group—Hispanic Americans.

Many Hispanics come to Oregon to work as seasonal agricultural workers. Many decide to remain in the state as permanent residents.

AN AFRICAN-AMERICAN HEROINE

One of the most distinguished members of Portland's early black community was Beatrice Morrow Cannaday, born in Texas in 1890. At the age of twenty she moved to Portland. She married the editor and co-founder of the *Portland Advocate*, the city's only African-American newspaper at the time. Within two years she was the paper's assistant editor, and in 1929 she became its editor.

By that time, Cannaday had become a leading figure in African-American affairs in Portland and beyond. In addition to attacking racial discrimination in her writing, she helped found the Portland chapter of the National Association for the Advancement of Colored People in 1914. After graduating from the Northwestern School of Law, Cannaday became the first black woman admitted to the practice of law in Oregon. She then helped write a civil-rights law that would have ended racial discrimination in public places. The law failed to pass, but Cannaday succeeded in her campaign to have the old "black laws" against African-American settlement and home ownership removed from the books.

Cannaday left Portland in the 1930s to settle in Los Angeles, where she remained until her death in 1974. She is remembered in Oregon, though, as an important part of the history of African Americans and of women in the state.

"There's more competition than I thought here, but you can still get good work," said Fermin Carillo of Mexico after moving to Gresham, just east of Portland. Heriberto Aguilar moved with his wife and children from Mexico City to Canby. At first it was hard for Aguilar to communicate in English. Now he makes time each week to work with young Hispanic men and women, helping them to feel at home in the United States.

The early years of the twenty-first century brought a wave of immigrants from Russia and nearby countries, such as Ukraine, Armenia, and Georgia. Many of these newcomers have settled on the east side of Portland, where dozens of small stores offer Russian and Eastern European groceries, movie rentals, and community newspapers in a variety of languages.

Immigration and ethnic diversity are reflected in Oregon's religious culture. As in the United States as a whole, the majority of Oregonians who identify themselves as religious belong to Christian faiths. The church with the most members statewide is the Roman Catholic Church, which has many Hispanic members, followed by the Church of Latter-Day Saints (the Mormons). Other Christian faiths in Oregon include Baptists, Methodists, and Presbyterians. Oregon's Jewish, Muslim, Hindu, and Buddhist communities represent a small part of the state's population—less than 1 percent for each religion—but each group appears to be growing as newcomers move into the state. Buddhism, especially, seems to be thriving, chiefly in Portland and Eugene.

One distinctive feature of religious life in Oregon is the unusually high percentage of people who describe themselves as "nonreligious." According to a 1990 survey by the City University of New York, about 17 percent of Oregonians fall into this group, compared with 7 percent for the United States as a whole.

Fighting Racism

Not everyone welcomes Oregon's growing diversity. A few young people called skinheads (because they shave their heads) have insulted or attacked people of color. African Americans and members of other minority groups have had to battle prejudice and hate crimes.

One hate crime in early 1996 attracted national attention. Two white students at Oregon State University in the small town of Corvallis were convicted of harassing a black student. Led by students, two thousand people came together to speak out against racism. The rally was one of the biggest meetings in the town's history.

Religious as well as cultural diversity is celebrated in Oregon.

Kids at Wilsonville High School south of Portland took action when racist graffiti started showing up on school walls. Fifteen-year-old Sarah Leitch passed out buttons with a simple but important message: RESPECT. Students also planned to put up a HATE-FREE ZONE banner. Sophomore Adam Wolff said, "Like Martin Luther King says, you have to change people's habits first before you change their hearts."

THE GOOD LIFE

Oregonians believe that their state offers them a good life. For many Oregonians, the good life is the outdoor life. "I'm not happy unless I'm on my board," says seventeen-year-old Curt Evans. He's talking about windsurfing—standing on a surfboard with a small sail and zipping across the choppy waters of the Columbia. Hood River, a tributary of the Columbia River, is one of the best places in the world for windsurfing. On good days the brightly colored sails of hundreds of boards dance across the blue water like a swarm of butterflies.

A windsurfer "catches air" on the Columbia River.

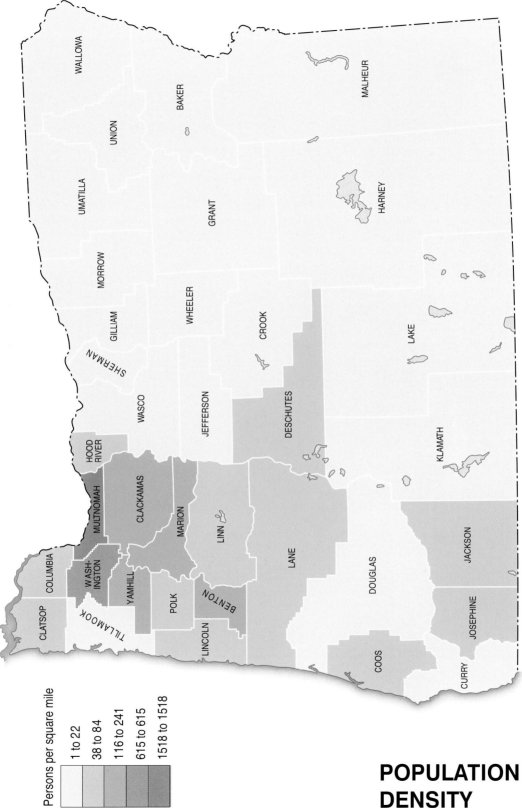

WALLOWA

BAKER

MALHEUR

UNION

HARNEY

UMATILLA

GRANT

MORROW

WHEELER

LAKE

GILLIAM

CROOK

SHERMAN

WASCO

JEFFERSON

DESCHUTES

KLAMATH

HOOD
RIVER

MULTNOMAH

CLACKAMAS

MARION

LINN

COLUMBIA

WASH-
INGTON

YAMHILL

LANE

JACKSON

CLATSOP

POLK

BENTON

DOUGLAS

TILLAMOOK

LINCOLN

JOSEPHINE

COOS

CURRY

Persons per square mile

1 to 22

38 to 84

116 to 241

615 to 615

1518 to 1518

**POPULATION
DENSITY**

CELEBRATING DIVERSITY

Ethnic groups share their heritage with other Oregonians in festivals large and small. On May 5, Mexico's national holiday, Portland celebrates with the Cinco de Mayo festival. Visitors munch on burritos and tacos, buy pottery and other Mexican handicrafts, and enjoy Mexico's magnificent folk dancers and singers.

Native Americans honor the traditions of the West at the Tygh Valley All-Indian Rodeo, held in The Dalles. They also hold a number of celebrations called powwows throughout the year in various parts of the state. German Americans and others enjoy the traditional German fall festival Oktoberfest in Mount Angel and the Sauerkraut Festival in Saint Helen's, where people enter cooking contests for bread, cake, and even ice cream made with sauerkraut! Portland has an annual Greek festival, while the Scandinavian Midsummer Festival takes place on the Oregon coast. The High Desert Celtic Festival, a celebration of Irish and Scottish culture, is held in Central Oregon.

Oregon has fourteen national forests that contain thirty-four wilderness areas. "What I love about my life here is that I'm never more than an hour or so from some kind of wilderness. Walking those trails, seeing the trees and the distant mountains, is the best exercise for your body and your spirit," says an Oregon-born woman who lives in Portland and hikes every weekend. A lot of people must agree with her. According to a survey in the early 1990s, Oregonians hike, camp, and ski more than most other Americans.

Settlers first came to Oregon to farm the fertile Willamette Valley. Today more Oregonians live in the Willamette Valley than on the coast, in the mountains, or in eastern Oregon. These days many more Oregonians live in cities or towns than on farms. Portland and its outlying communities are growing fast. Salem and Eugene, both in the Willamette Valley, are major cities. Salem is the state's center of government, and Eugene is an important educational center. Other important cities include Newport on the coast, Medford and Klamath Falls in the south, The Dalles on the Columbia River,

The city of Newport, found on Oregon's central coast, is a community of over nine thousand people that claims to be "the friendliest" city in the state.

and Pendleton in the east. Bend, in Central Oregon, is one of the state's fastest-growing communities. Close to mountains, rivers, and high desert, Bend offers a multitude of opportunities for outdoor recreation. It has lured young people who love the outdoor life as well as retirees and telecommuters.

Small-town life is still a big part of Oregon culture, however. "Portland's okay, I guess, but here I know all my neighbors," said a resident of tiny Troutdale, a town near the Columbia Gorge. A couple who left good jobs in Portland to open a store in much smaller Prineville explained, "A smaller town is a good place for our kids. They'll be close to nature, and they'll have fewer chances to get into trouble."

Some small towns are growing a bit as people leave Portland and out-of-state cities for a slower, more relaxed way of life. "One of the things I love best of all is no phones," says Patty Baca, who lives in Granite, population twenty-four. Granite is one of many Wallowa Mountain ghost towns, left behind when the local gold rush ended years ago. "Granite is not so much of a ghost town anymore," Baca says. "A lot of people are moving in and building. I think we've got three or four new people a year. It's a boomtown."

PROBLEMS IN PARADISE

Two important elements of a good life are health care and education. Traditionally, Oregonians are strong supporters of public schools. They also created programs to extend health care to all citizens. However, health care and education suffered when the state's income fell short of the money needed to maintain them.

Before the late 1990s, Oregon was considered a pioneer in health-care reform. The state's government created the Oregon Health Plan to pay for health care for unemployed Oregonians or those with low incomes. The

During the mid-1800s and the gold rush, Jacksonville, Oregon, was home to miners seeking their fortune. Today the town is a National Historic Landmark retaining its small town charm.

Chapter Four

A Leader in Lawmaking

Even before Oregon was a U.S. territory, its settlers wanted to be governed by law. In 1843 a hundred settlers met on the Willamette River to form their own government. Dr. Robert Newell was one of them. He wrote, "After a few days' experience I became satisfied that I knew as little about the business of legislating as the majority of my colleagues."

Despite their lack of experience, the settlers managed to elect a sheriff and governor and to set up a government. They lay the foundation for modern lawmaking in Oregon.

INSIDE GOVERNMENT

Oregon's modern state government, like the settlers' government, is modeled on the federal government of the United States. The state government has three branches: executive, judicial, and legislative.

Executive

The executive branch of the Oregon government is responsible for carrying out every state function, from running the public schools to picking up litter along the highways. The executive branch includes six elected officials:

The State Capitol Building in Salem houses the legislative branch of the government, as well as the governor, the secretary of state, and the state treasurer.

governor, secretary of state, treasurer, attorney general, commissioner of labor and industries, and superintendent of public instruction. These officials oversee several agencies and thousands of employees.

Judicial

Law cases are heard and decided in four different types of courts. Most trials, including criminal and juvenile trials, are heard in one of the state's thirty-six circuit courts in twenty-seven districts. These courts have a total of 166 judges. Cases involving tax law are heard in the Tax Court.

The Oregon Court of Appeals has ten judges. They rule on appeals, or challenges, to the decisions of the lower courts. The Oregon Supreme Court, with seven judges, is the state's highest court. All judges of Oregon courts are elected by voters to six-year terms. Cases involving federal laws are heard in federal courts.

Legislative

The legislative branch of the government is responsible for making laws, deciding how the state's money is to be spent, and debating public issues. The Legislative Assembly meets in Salem, the state capital. It has two parts: a senate and a house of representatives. Oregon has thirty state senators, each elected for four years. It has sixty state representatives, who are elected for two-year terms. Oregon voters also send two senators and five representatives to Congress in Washington, D.C.

Oregon's thirty state senators meet in the Senate Chambers in the State Capitol Building. The hanging mural by Frank H. Schwarz depicts the celebration of Oregon's statehood in 1859.

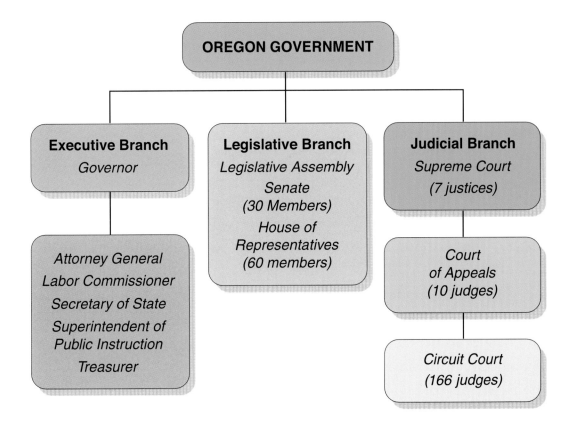

OREGON GOVERNMENT

Executive Branch
Governor

Attorney General
Labor Commissioner
Secretary of State
Superintendent of
Public Instruction
Treasurer

Legislative Branch
Legislative Assembly
Senate
(30 Members)
House of
Representatives
(60 members)

Judicial Branch
Supreme Court
(7 justices)

Court
of Appeals
(10 judges)

Circuit Court
(166 judges)

In 1992 the people of Oregon voted to limit the amount of time officials could stay in public office. Officials' terms would be limited to a maximum of six to twelve years, depending upon the office. Supporters of this controversial term limits measure claimed that it would remove stuck-in-a-rut "career" politicians and make room for eager new public servants. Others disagreed, however, and challenged the measure in court.

In 2002 the Oregon Supreme Court ruled that the term limits measure was unconstitutional because of the way it had been worded. Those who favor term limits for state legislators will try again to get such a measure made into law.

CITIZEN LAWMAKERS

Oregon has a history of making progressive laws that right injustices or are ahead of their time. Between 1902 and 1908 Oregon passed a series of laws to make elections and lawmaking more democratic. Soon other states adopted "the Oregon system."

Election reform involved the direct primary, which allows Oregonians to vote for candidates in the primary elections, in which party members choose their party's candidate for the general election. Earlier, people voted for the party of their choice, and party officials selected the candidates. Another reform gave voters the right to recall public officials, or remove them from office.

The most important reforms, however, were the initiative and the referendum. The initiative is a way for ordinary citizens to make new laws or changes to the state constitution. These new ideas, or initiatives, are included on the ballots of state elections. If the voters approve them, they go to the state legislature for action. The referendum lets any citizen ask the people of Oregon to vote for or against an action by the state government.

People who want to put their initiatives and referenda on the ballot must first collect a certain number of signatures from voters. Groups that support the initiatives send dozens or even hundreds of signature gatherers to public places such as mall parking

Primary election voters wait in line to cast their vote at a ballot drop site in downtown Portland.

lots and city squares. Some Oregonians have grown tired of hearing, "Will you sign my petition?" four or five times a day during election season. "These petition people are a real nuisance," complained Sue Fleming while she shopped in downtown Portland. "I've had to brush them away like flies."

Oregonians have voted on initiatives dealing with the environment, pay and benefits for state employees such as teachers, and many other issues. One of the most wide-reaching initiatives in the state's history was Measure 5, which appeared on the 1990 ballot. In the years since voters approved that initiative, Measure 5 has had a major impact on life in Oregon.

Measure 5 set a limit on property taxes. It pleased people who worried that taxes on real estate were becoming too high, but at the same time, it lowered the amount of money available for schools and other government services. It is one reason for the budget crisis in the state's public health-care and school programs.

Many public services have been cut back since Measure 5 passed. When universities began receiving less money from the state, they raised tuition. Some of Oregon's state parks closed, while others raised their admission fees. Libraries shortened their hours and dropped some programs. One unhappy librarian said, "Sure, Measure 5 saved property owners a few dollars today, but what are we doing to our future?"

One result of Measure 5 is that, with property taxes limited, the state government has had to look for other sources of income. One source is state-sponsored gambling in the form of lotteries and games of chance, such as video poker. As state-sponsored gambling has increased, so have the problems of people who gamble irresponsibly or have become addicted to gambling. Some Oregonians have criticized the state for relying on this source of income. Yet the money earned by the state lottery is part of what keeps schools, parks, and other public services afloat all across Oregon.

Income from the Oregon lottery has helped the economy by creating jobs and financing public education, national parks, and salmon habitats.

No one is sure what the long-term effects of Measure 5 will be. As a landowner who voted for the measure said, "Hey, the state listened to what the people want. That's democracy in action." Others point out that the shortage of money for schools, health programs, and other public services cannot be blamed just on Measure 5. The general downturn of the U.S. economy in the late 1990s and early 2000s affected Oregon as well.

OREGON BY COUNTY

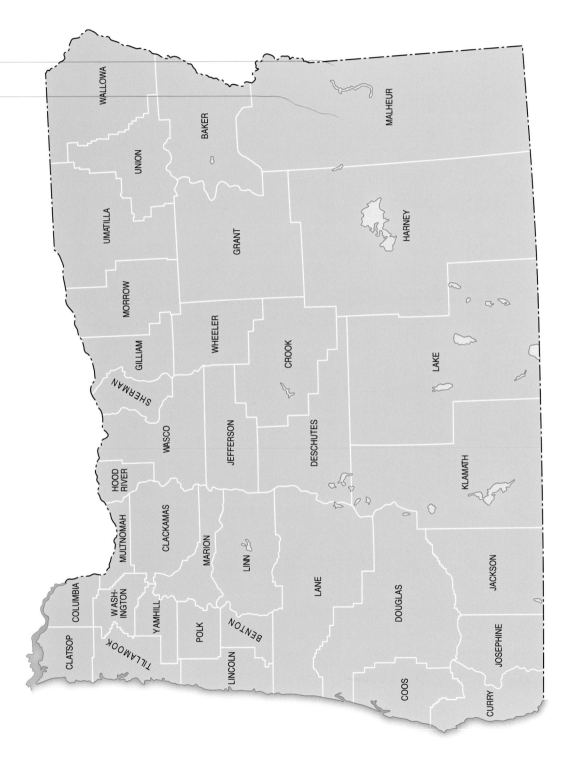

CONFLICTS AND CHALLENGES

Oregonians have as many different points of view on public affairs as Oregon has scenic viewpoints along its highways and byways—and Oregon has a lot of scenic viewpoints. The economic downturn of the late 1990s and early 2000s deepened conflicts among Oregon's various population groups. At one point John Kitzhaber, governor of Oregon from 1995 to 2003, described the state as "ungovernable."

What makes uniting Oregon such a challenge is that the state has attracted so many new residents from other places. From the earliest days of pioneer settlement, Oregon's original inhabitants, the Native Americans, have been forced to cope with changes brought about by outsiders coming into their homeland. Today, old-time non-Indian Oregonians, especially in rural districts and small towns, have a history in the state that may go three or four generations into the past. To many of them, Oregon is defined by logging, agriculture, and ranching.

Most of the newer residents, however, have settled in the cities and work in office jobs. Many of them were drawn to Oregon by its natural beauty. Committed to environmental causes, they tend to support conservation rules that rural Oregonians, such as the inhabitants of the former timber towns, view as destructive to their livelihoods.

Adding to the challenge of governing Oregon is the system of initiatives and referenda. Although Oregon's government gives the people a direct voice in shaping the laws of their state, it also challenges the state to enforce laws and regulations that sometimes work against each other.

In 2004, for example, Oregon voters passed an initiative that may influence the state's future even more than Measure 5 has. Called Measure 37, it concerns the conflict between property owners' rights and laws designed to protect trees, streams, wetlands, and other environmental features.

Environmental protection is an issue on which many Oregonians openly voice their views.

Under Measure 37, if environmental regulations hurt the commercial value of a piece of land, the property's owner can demand that the state government pay the difference. If, for example, regulations protecting a wetland kept a property owner from having his land developed into a mall or parking lot, the state would have to pay the property owner the lost value—or let the development proceed.

Supporters of Measure 37 claim that it gives property owners fair treatment. Those who oppose it fear that it will clog the courts with demands for claims, and that it will lead to suburban sprawl and unregulated development. For a long time, many Oregonians have taken pride in the green spaces around Portland and other cities. Time will tell how green Oregon can remain.

Chapter Five

Making a Living

The 1980s brought an economic boom to Oregon. The state's economy grew faster than the overall U.S. economy. Starting in 1991, however, layoffs and the arrival of new workers produced a job shortage. By the end of the decade, unemployment was rising fast.

Like many other parts of the United States, Oregon endured a general downturn of its economy during the early 2000s. Companies cut jobs or transferred them overseas. Some employers went out of business or moved to other regions. By 2003 Oregon had the nation's highest rate of unemployment. About 8.2 percent of its workers were jobless, compared with 5.4 percent for the country as a whole.

Fortunately for Oregonians, things began to look up when the economy showed signs of improvement the following year. Some new jobs were created, and people returned to work. By late 2004, Oregon's unemployment rate had dropped to 6.8 percent—still higher than the national average, but not by much.

Prosperity and hard times seem to come and go in cycles for individual regions and states as well as for the entire country. "We survived

Forestry is Oregon's number-one industry, but it now contributes much less to the economy than services and retail trade do.

A WINGDING IN SALEM

Late summer is state fair time in the capital city of Salem. People from around the state gather on the fairgrounds for a wide variety of events. A day at the fair can include South American music, sheep and cattle shows, a Spam recipe contest, Japanese sumo wrestling, a laser light show, and performances by entertainers like Bill Cosby.

Kids can become stars of the fair. In 1995 twelve-year-old Sterling Holmes won a cooking contest with his recipe for corn nachos. His prize was a mountain bike and a helmet. That same year, fifteen-year-old Robin Marsh won two blue ribbons for her brown-and-white guernsey cows.

More than two thousand people work at the eleven-day fair. Attendance has dropped a bit in recent years, but the state fair is still a lively Oregon tradition.

a much worse depression once before," said eighty-seven-year-old Margaret Sammons, a lifelong Portland resident, referring to the Great Depression of the 1930s. "When we look back on this last few years, they don't seem so bad, do they?"

WORKING IN OREGON

Oregon's economy was traditionally based on resources from the land, rather than on manufacturing. Over time, however, the economy has become more diversified. Jobs that provide services, especially for tourists, are the biggest part of the economy. Services, including retail trade, account for more than 80 percent of the state's yearly economic production.

OREGON WORKFORCE

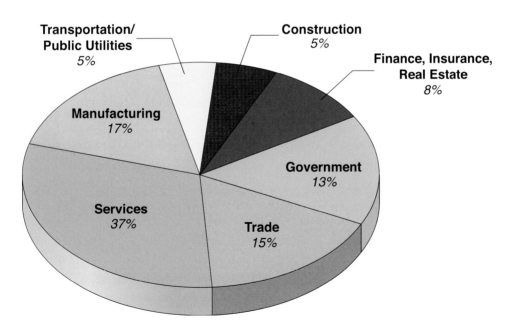

Native Americans in Oregon, as in other states, have found a new source of income in recent years. Under laws that permit gambling-based businesses on tribal land, a number of tribes have opened casinos. With restaurants and musical acts as well as gambling, the casinos draw thousands of visitors. The casinos' profits benefit the tribes, but not all Native Americans approve of them. Some feel that gambling is a poor basis for an economy.

The same argument can be made against one of the state's key sources of income: state-sponsored gambling in the form of lotteries and video poker. These games bring money into the state treasury, helping to provide funds for education and services such as maintenance of state parks. Yet they have also created serious problems for Oregonians who have become addicted to gambling.

Additional businesses in Oregon have given rise to controversy. The Nike Corporation, which sells athletic shoes and clothing, is a global business giant. Its headquarters are located just outside Portland. Some activists have accused Nike of unfair or oppressive business practices—such as paying low wages for long hours of work—in the foreign countries where much of the company's manufacturing takes place.

Also located near Portland is a major manufacturing center for Intel, a maker of silicon chips and other computer parts. Intel has been a big part of the growth of Oregon's high-technology industry, which flourished in the 1980s and contributed to the state's economic boom. Intel isn't alone. So many computer, software, and other high-tech businesses have set up operations in the Willamette Valley south of Portland that the area is called Oregon's Silicon Forest—a reference to Silicon Valley, a famous high-tech area in California.

One of Oregon's leading economic growth sectors is the high-tech industry, which produces computer parts and microchips.

Forest Products

Forestry dominated Oregon's economy throughout the twentieth century. The timber industry cuts trees, ships logs, and turns them into boards, chips, cardboard, or paper at mills. Forestry remains Oregon's leading industry, followed by agriculture and tourism.

Although Oregon is the largest supplier of lumber and plywood in the United States, the timber industry has had problems in recent years. Workers blame environmentalists for cutbacks in logging and the loss of timber jobs. Laws that protect forest areas have certainly hurt logging, but there are other reasons why jobs are vanishing from timber towns throughout Oregon.

Almost half of Oregon is covered with forest, contributing to the state's historic role as a leader in the manufacturing of lumber, wood, pulp, and paper products.

Take Reedsport, a coastal community of about five thousand people. In early 1999 International Paper (IP) closed its Gardiner mill and sold its holdings in Pacific Northwest forests there, thus wiping out about three hundred jobs. IP said it had closed the mill because the company already had on hand more finished products than it was selling. In addition, IP could make its products more cheaply in the South than in the Northwest.

Reedsport was hit hard. The town's major source of employment was gone. "A lot of people are looking for the mill to start," said Mayor Ted Walters. "But there are a lot of people also saying, 'I'm out of here.'" Carol Harris, a local bartender, feared that a permanent shutdown of the mill "would make a ghost town out of this place."

Some people who have worked at the mill all their lives are going in new directions. "I consider my future down at IP, so I have to start over again at thirty-eight," said Mark Bedard, who plans to study business administration at a community college. He will receive financial aid from a federal job-training program for displaced workers. Felicia Bitek, a mill worker who wants to become an electrician, also applied for the program. "Going down there and getting tested after twenty years out of high school, I was very nervous," she said. She signed up for classes in math, computers, and blueprint reading.

The timber industry faces an uncertain future. Timber workers, and whole timber towns, are trying to do what Felicia Bitek did. Many realize that to survive, they will have to change.

One example of change can be found in Oakridge, a town long dependent on the timber industry. Randy Drelling, president of the Oakridge Chamber of Commerce and owner of an outdoor-adventures company, is demonstrating that recreational activities such as mountain biking can attract visitors and provide new sources of income for the community.

2002 GROSS STATE PRODUCT: $115 Million

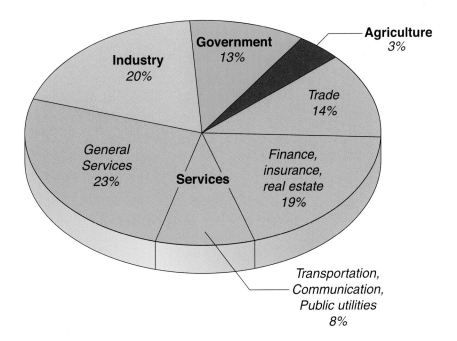

Agriculture

Agriculture is Oregon's second-largest industry. The state produces wheat, of course, but it is also the nation's top producer of some more unusual crops, such as Christmas trees, grass seed, hazelnuts, peppermint, and raspberries and blackberries. Farms and orchards yield large crops of strawberries, onions, cauliflower, prunes, apples, pears, and nursery and greenhouse plants.

Wheat farming is found mostly in the north central region of Oregon. Much of the wheat grown is exported to Asian countries.

FROSTY FRUIT SMOOTHIE

What's a marionberry? It's a cross between a raspberry and a black-berry, and it grows only in Oregon. One of the best ways to enjoy this sweet-tart berry is in a frosty fruit smoothie. Don't worry if you can't find marionberries at your grocery store; just use raspberries or blackberries—or both—instead.

1. Peel two bananas, wrap them in plastic wrap, and put them in the freezer. Also wrap and freeze 1 cup of fresh berries (or buy ones that are already frozen). Leave the bananas and berries in the freezer for twenty-four hours.

2. Pour one cup of apple juice into a blender. Add the bananas. Blend at high speed. Now add the berries and blend again until the mixture is smooth. It should be as thick as a milkshake. If it's too thick, add a little more juice. Makes two servings.

Ships carry Oregon's agricultural exports around the world. South Korea, Japan, the Philippines, Pakistan, Saudi Arabia, and other countries buy its french fries, wheat, and grass seed.

The cattle industry contributes several hundred million dollars each year to the state's economy. Dairy farming and hay making are also big business, especially in western Oregon. The Tillamook Valley, a low-lying plain covered with lush green grass, is a dairy cow's paradise and the center of the state's cheese industry. When the valley turned into a vast lake during the floods of 1996, farmers and volunteers worked desperately to save the cows. Still, many farmers lost their livestock.

Cows graze on the fertile Oregon land. Beef and dairy cattle make up a large percentage of Oregon's agricultural income.

Oregon's natural attractions draw tourist dollars into the state.

Tourism

Tourism is a big industry in Oregon. It includes restaurants, hotels and motels, museums, recreational businesses, transportation, and more. The Pacific Northwest has become a popular vacation spot, and Oregon's economy is relying more and more on tourist dollars. By the mid-2000s tourism was bringing more than $5 billion a year to Oregon. The state's tourism office has ten welcome centers throughout the state to help visitors make the most of their vacations.

Why do people come to Oregon? "This place has everything!" said Jeff Margulies, a fourteen-year-old from New York, during his first visit to the state. "You can go snowboarding on Mount Hood in the middle of summer, and the same day you can go whitewater rafting. Plus it's real clean here."

EARNING A LIVING

Natural Resources
- Diatomite
- Forests
- Limestone
- Natural Gas
- Sand, gravel
- Soil

Manufacturing
- Electrical equipment
- Food processing
- Lumber
- Machinery
- Paper products
- Printing
- Scientific instruments

Agriculture
- Beef Cattle
- Cranberries
- Dairy Cattle
- Forest Products
- Grass Seed
- Sheep
- Wheat

Snake R.

Joseph

Baker

La Grande

Pendleton

Umatilla

Columbia R.

The Dalles

Gresham

Oregon City

Silverton

Marion

Lebanon

Albany

Corvallis

Toledo

Salem

Beaverton

Hillsboro

Portland

St. Helens

Astoria

Lincoln City

Eugene

Springfield

Madras

John Day R.

Bend

Burns

Ontario

Malheur R.

Powder R.

Grande Ronde R.

Owyhee R.

Deschutes R.

Willamette R.

Umpqua R.

Roseburg

North Bend

Brookings

Grants Pass

Medford

Ashland

Klamath Falls

Altamont

Minerals and Energy

Gold is still mined in central and eastern Oregon and in the southern mountains. Some miners work their claims alone, like the old-time prospectors. Other mines are run by multimillion-dollar corporations. Environmentalists have raised concerns about pollution caused by these large operations, some of which use poisonous chemicals to treat the gold ore.

With both beaches and rocky mountains, Oregon is a good source of sand, gravel, and stone for road making and building. These materials are used locally and also exported to other states and nations.

Oregon's natural-gas reserves will provide energy for the future, but the state also makes better use of renewable resources than any other state. One-quarter of all energy used in Oregon comes from hydroelectric power or from burning wood. Many people use solar or wind energy in their homes, and businesses are beginning to use these renewable, pollution-free resources as well.

SHAPING THE FUTURE

Although forestry remains Oregon's top industry, it is no longer growing. Oregon must increasingly rely on other economic activities. The state's leaders hope that high-technology firms will play an even greater role in the state economy. They realize, though, that if Oregon is to attract such companies and their highly educated workers, the state must solve some of the problems with its school systems and other services.

Another business that may play an increasing role in Oregon's economic future is international shipping. For decades Portland was a major seaport. Its importance declined in the late twentieth century,

The Columbia River is used heavily in the exporting of wheat. During the late 1990s, $13 billion worth of cargo was shipped through this waterway.

however, because the shipping channel in the Columbia River was too shallow for some of the largest container ships. Sea traffic shifted to other ports, threatening to leave Portland high and dry.

In the early 2000s work began on a project to deepen the Columbia shipping channel. Before long a South Korean shipping company announced that it would increase its business in the Port of Portland. The company's ships will keep Portland connected with ports in Japan, a leading customer for Oregon hay, potatoes, and other agricultural products. State economic planner hope that other shipping companies, such as those that move manufactured goods from China to the United States, will help Portland carve out a solid place in the global economy.

Chapter Six

Oregon Road Trip

"Oregon is one of the coolest states we've seen," said Heather McDonald, who has toured twenty-three states in her family's camper. "I want to come back again so I can see everything here!"

Lots of people feel the same way. Oregonians like traveling around their state as much as visitors do. Any tour of Oregon should start with Portland, Oregon's largest city and center of cultural activities.

A CITY OF MANY NAMES

Portland has grown a lot since 1845, when Asa Lovejoy and Francis Pettygrove flipped their coin to choose its name. Back then Portland was a small landing area on the west side of the Willamette River—but it soon began sprawling out in all directions. In the early days people called the city Stumptown because so many stumps were left standing where trees had been cut down to make room for roads and buildings.

Docks and warehouses were built along the river to handle the city's shipping trade. Although shipping has declined somewhat, Portland is still a harbor town. The skyline along the river bristles with cargo cranes, and

Oregon's sights and sounds can be captured by a drive along scenic Highway 101.

Ships anchor along the Willamette River in Portland.

grain barges and tankers ply the waters of the Columbia. Occasionally, cruise ships come a few miles up the Willamette to dock in downtown Portland. Smaller craft, such as pleasure boats and kayaks, dot the waters of the Willamette as it runs through the city.

Early Portlanders who grew wealthy built large homes on the forested hills west of downtown. Immigrants and working-class people settled in neighborhoods north and south of the city center. Soon people were living and working on the east side of the Willamette, too.

At first, the only way to get from one side of Portland to the other was by ferry. Then, in 1887, Portlanders built the first of many bridges across the river. The bridge's owners charged five cents each for people, sheep, and hogs to cross. Today ten bridges span the river in Portland, which is sometimes called the City of Bridges. Anyone can cross them for free—but it has been a long time since a sheep or a hog tried to do so.

City of Roses is another of Portland's nicknames. Roses grow extremely well in the mild, moist climate of western Oregon, and the city is full of gardens that burst with their colors and scents. The International Rose Test Gardens, perched on a hill with a splendid view of Portland's skyline, is a flower lover's paradise with more than ten thousand rose bushes.

Roses are the theme of Portland's biggest annual event, the Rose Festival, which runs for nearly a month and includes dozens of activities, such as balloon rides, auto and boat races, and fireworks. The highlight of the festival is the Grand Floral Parade of floats decorated with flowers. It is the second-largest floral parade in the United States.

City of Fountains might be another good nickname for Portland. Downtown Portland is a mix of dazzling modern office towers—the tallest is the Wells Fargo Center at forty-one stories—and small, inviting shops, coffee bars, and restaurants on almost every street. Scattered among the downtown blocks are half a dozen fountains, including one that was built to look like a mountain waterfall. On hot days kids play in the fountains.

Among Portland's major attractions are the zoo, the art museum, and the World

Thirteen thousand gallons of water per minute flow over the terraces of the Ira C. Keller Fountain in Portland.

Forestry Center. The Oregon Zoo is the state's biggest paid attraction. It has arctic tundra and Pacific Northwest wildlife exhibits and much more. At Zoo Concerts, Portlanders picnic on a grassy lawn while folk, blues, and jazz musicians perform and elephants sway to the music. The Portland Art Museum, in the heart of downtown Portland, has collections of Native American, Asian, and African art as well as European and American artwork. More than 45,000 schoolchildren take part in the museum's programs for young people each year.

Kids also like the Oregon Museum of Science and Industry in southeast Portland. A real submarine, interactive science experiments, an IMAX theater, and a planetarium are just a few of its attractions.

Many Oregon museums focus on history. In Portland the museum of the Oregon Historical Society features exhibits on all parts of Oregon's past. In nearby Oregon City, the End of the Oregon Trail Interpretive Center is a museum about the Oregon Trail. Every summer the center hosts a play called *Oregon Fever*, which captures the excitement of the settlers' journey west.

Portland is full of things to see and do—but so is the rest of the state. The Willamette Valley south of Portland has quiet back roads through gentle farm country. People now grow grapes and make wine in this part of Oregon, and winery tours are popular.

Visitors to Salem can tour the state capitol or stroll through neighborhoods where historic buildings have been preserved. One building, the home of missionary Jason Lee, was built in 1841. It is the oldest frame house in the Northwest.

A little to the west is the small town of Monmouth, home of the Paul Jensen Arctic Museum. It is the only arctic museum in the lower

The heart of wine-making country in Oregon is the Willamette Valley. Its climate of warm summers, mild winters, and wet springs produce grapes perfect for wine making.

forty-eight states and has more than three thousand items related to the peoples of the arctic. Fifty thousand people have visited the museum since it opened in 1985.

THE COAST

Oregon has nearly four hundred miles of coastline—"the most beautiful in the world," insisted a teenage girl from Florence. Pictures of Oregon's towering offshore rocks, misty capes, and curving beaches show up regularly on scenic calendars. One of the best things about the Oregon coast is that it belongs to everyone. In 1967 the state legislature passed the "beach bill," which opened all beaches to the public.

PLACES TO SEE

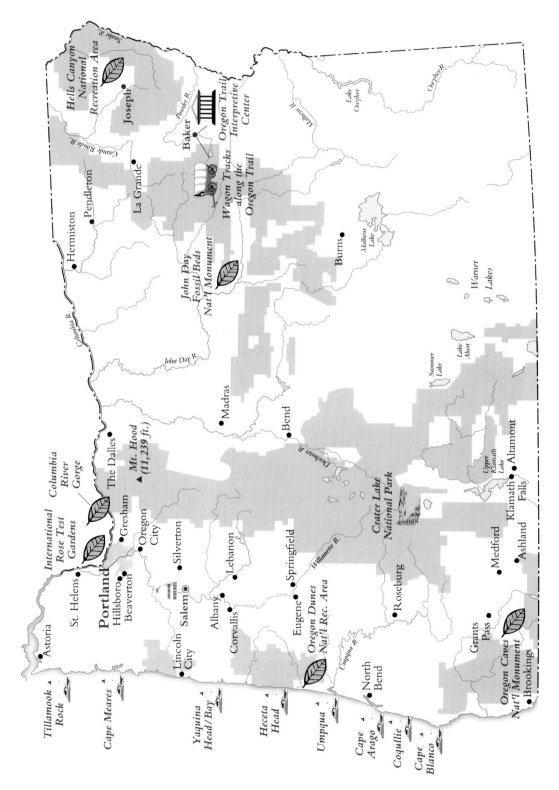

Hells Canyon National Recreation Area

Snake R.

Joseph

Grande Ronde R.

Ponder R.

Baker

Oregon Trail Interpretive Center

Wagon Tracks along the Oregon Trail

Malheur R.

Lake Owyhee

Owyhee R.

Pendleton

La Grande

Hermiston

John Day Fossil Beds Nat'l Monument

Burns

Malheur Lake

Warner Lakes

Columbia R.

John Day R.

Madras

Bend

Deschutes R.

Summer Lake

Lake Abert

Mt. Hood (11,239 ft.)

The Dalles

Columbia River Gorge

International Rose Test Gardens

Gresham

Oregon City

Silverton

Willamette R.

Crater Lake National Park

Upper Klamath Lake

Altamont

Klamath Falls

Portland

St. Helens

Hillsboro

Beaverton

Salem

Albany

Lebanon

Corvallis

Springfield

Eugene

Oregon Dunes Nat'l Rec. Area

Roseburg

Medford

Ashland

Astoria

Lincoln City

Umpqua R.

North Bend

Grants Pass

Oregon Caves Nat'l Monument

Brookings

Tillamook Rock

Cape Meares

Yaquina Head/Bay

Heceta Head

Umpqua

Cape Arago

Coquille

Cape Blanco

Named for a cannon found on the beach in 1846, Cannon Beach attracts visitors by its natural beauty.

Astoria, at the north end of the coast, was the first permanent settlement in the American West. One of the town's modern attractions is the Columbia River Maritime Museum, a tribute to the region's seafaring history. Nearby is a replica of Fort Clatsop, where the Lewis and Clark expedition spent the winter of 1805–1806.

Lincoln City and Newport, two of the largest communities on the central coast, are full of shops and restaurants for visitors who come there year-round. The Oregon Coast Aquarium in Newport, with a big shark tank and exhibits of Pacific undersea life, has become a leading attraction for visitors. You don't have to go to a museum to see ocean life, however. Along this stretch of coast are cliffs and capes where people gather to watch majestic grey whales swim by on their yearly migrations. The whales swim south in December and January and north with their young in April and May.

Most of Oregon's coast is craggy and rocky. Between Florence and North Bend, however, is the forty-mile-long Oregon Dunes National Recreation Area, a sweep of rolling white sand dunes. Farther south are Coos Bay, the largest city on the coast, and Bandon, which is the "storm-watching capital of Oregon" and the "cranberry capital of Oregon."

HEADING INLAND

Southern Oregon has something for everyone. Rafters and kayakers from all over the country come to the Rogue River, one of the Wild and Scenic Waterways chosen by Congress for protection against dams and development. The Rogue and other rivers in the area also offer salmon and steelhead trout fishing.

GOING UNDERGROUND

Highway 199 leads south through Oregon's redwood country. It passes through the small town of Cave Junction, the gateway to the Oregon Caves National Monument. In 1874 Elijah Davidson and his dog Bruno were high in the hills of southern Oregon, chasing a bear, when Bruno seemed to vanish. The dog had discovered the entrance to one of the most spectacular cave systems in the United States. More than 4 million people have toured the caves since President William H. Taft declared them a national monument in 1909. "Caveman weddings," with the barefoot bride and groom dressed in furs, used to be held deep in the caves. Today, people experience the Oregon Caves through guided tours of the glistening marble formations and echoing caverns.

There are more than ninety miles of trails in Crater Lake National Park. Hikers can explore the crater's rim on its Cleetwood Trail.

The town of Ashland, nestled in the southern mountains, is the site of Oregon's most famous theater event: the annual Oregon Shakespeare Festival. Each year, from February through October, actors perform eleven plays, five of which are by Shakespeare. The festival, which has won many dramatic awards, brings thousands of visitors to southern Oregon.

Most visitors to Ashland make time to visit Crater Lake National Park to see the deepest lake in the United States. For years people have tried to describe the dazzling dark blue color of the lake's water. A visitor in 1854 called it "the bluest water I ever saw." He thought the lake ought to be called

Mysterious Lake or Deep Blue Lake. Poet Walt Curtis described the color this way: "Water mirrors blue sky . . . Lonesome blue planet earth."

Crossing the Cascades, travelers enter central and eastern Oregon. Highway 395 from Lakeview to Burns passes through the "Oregon outback," a rugged region of mountains, deserts, and lakeside wetlands. Wildlife and fossils outnumber people in this part of the state.

Farther northeast are the Wallowa Mountains and Hells Canyon. A drive to the town of Joseph, named for the Nez Percé leader, heads into the heart of the mountains, where a monument to the chief stands on the shore of Wallowa Lake. Forest roads, closed in winter because of snow, run east to the rim of Hells Canyon and a mile-deep view.

TEN LARGEST CITIES

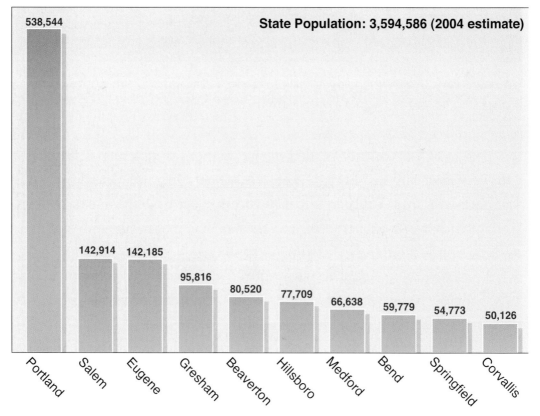

State Population: 3,594,586 (2004 estimate)

Portland	538,544
Salem	142,914
Eugene	142,185
Gresham	95,816
Beaverton	80,520
Hillsboro	77,709
Medford	66,638
Bend	59,779
Springfield	54,773
Corvallis	50,126

WHAT KIND OF NAME IS THAT?

Weird names are sprinkled across the map of Oregon. Take Helix, a tiny town in the northeast. Legend says it was named by an early resident who had an earache. His doctor told him that a part of his ear called the helix was infected. He liked the name and used it for the town.

How would you like to live in a town called Boring? "This is really *not* a dull place!" one citizen of Boring insisted, explaining that the town was named after old-time resident W. H. Boring. Remote, a tiny community near the coast, got its name because it is far away from other settlements.

Donner und Blitzen Creek, which flows into Malheur Lake, was not named for two of Santa's tiny reindeer. In 1864 army troops crossed the creek in a thunderstorm and gave it the German name for "thunder and lightning."

Many Oregon place-names are Indian words. *Yakso* is a Chinook word meaning "hair." The seventy-foot Yakso Falls on the Little River resemble a woman's long, flowing hair. Central Oregon has a town, a lake, a mountain, and a creek named Paulina, but they weren't named for some lonely settler's sweetheart. Paulina, or Paunina, was a chieftain of the Snake Indians who fought settlers in the 1860s.

You can find more place-names and the stories behind them in a book called *Oregon Geographic Names*, by Lewis A. McArthur.

Between the Wallowas and the Columbia River is Pendleton. This part of Oregon is filled with museums and historic markers that recall the days when the Oregon Trail passed through. These include the Oregon Trail Interpretive Center in Baker City; the Museum at Warm Springs, a reservation museum that showcases a stunning collection of tribal artifacts; and the Tamastslikt Cultural Center in Pendelton, which highlights the Cayuse, Umatilla, and Walla Walla cultures.

This part of Central Oregon is also sheep country, and Pendleton is a wool-processing center. The world-famous Pendleton wool blankets, usually decorated with Western or Indian designs, are made here. Pendleton is also the site of one of the biggest rodeos in the United States, the Pendleton Round-Up, a weeklong event held every September.

Central Oregon offers a window into the distant past. In the nineteenth century, scientists began finding fossils by the thousands along the John Day River. Today the John Day Fossil Beds National Monument protects three fossil fields. Visitors are welcome to tour them, but they can't expect to see dinosaur bones. The fossils found here are relics of plants, turtles, rhinos, bear-dogs, pigs, and horses that lived between 45 and 5 million years ago.

Beginning in 1910, the Pendleton Round-Up has been entertaining visitors with bronc riding, horse races, calf roping, and Native American culture.

The John Day fossil fields contain the preserved remains of plants and animals dating to the Cenozoic Era, the age of mammals and flowering plants.

Bend is Central Oregon's biggest city. Outdoor recreation has grown into one of the region's most important businesses, and Bend and the nearby town of Redmond have grown along with it. The two towns sell supplies and services to people who want to ski at Mount Bachelor, raft or kayak the Deschutes River's white water, or hike and camp in the Deschutes and Ochoco National Forests.

Rock climbers from all over the world test their skill at nearby Smith Rock State Park, where spires and cliffs rise sheer above the canyon of the Crooked River. People who don't climb like Smith Rock, too. They can stroll comfortable pathways and watch the climbers creep up the red rock walls like brightly colored spiders.

Several hours' drive north of Bend, the Columbia River flows through the majestic Columbia River Gorge, a National Scenic Area. "I've seen just about every part of Oregon," says Portlander Jim Schull, "and the gorge is still my favorite." The wide river winds between hills and cliffs that change from sunbaked golden brown in the east to mossy green in the west. There are more than a dozen waterfalls on Oregon's side of the gorge. Multnomah Falls is the state's highest, at 620 feet. A narrow scenic highway takes visitors over arched bridges and through tunnels up to Crown Point, a lookout on one of the highest spots in the gorge. To the southeast Mount Hood rears its pointed crown. To the southwest lies Portland, where our journey began.

Oregonians can't decide whether to show off their state or keep it to themselves. They are proud of Oregon, and they welcome the money that tourists bring to the state. At the same time, they are afraid that too many people will move to Oregon and ruin it. Tom McCall, a former governor of Oregon, used to say, "Visit our state of enchantment—but for heaven's sakes, don't stay!"

In 1980 McCall said that Oregon was becoming more crowded and that Oregonians were complaining that the future didn't look as bright as it used to. Then he added that if Oregonians make the right decisions, "we can still live on in a way that will let us boast, 'You bet, the future is what it used to be.'"

Multnomah Falls is the second highest waterfall in the United States that falls year-round. Visitors can cross between its two cataracts on the Benson Bridge.

THE FLAG: The flag was adopted in 1925. It displays a special version of the gold state seal on a navy blue background. On the flag, the words State of Oregon and the date 1859 from the state seal have been enlarged.

THE SEAL: The state seal was adopted in 1859, the year Oregon became a state. Just inside the seal border are thirty-three stars representing Oregon as the thirty-third state. The stars enclose a shield topped by the federal eagle. The British ship leaving and American ship arriving show that Oregon was never controlled by a foreign government. The ox-drawn wagon beneath the ships stands for the settlement of Oregon by means of the Oregon Trail. The trees, grain, farmer's plow, and miner's pick represent the state's natural resources and industries.

State Survey

Statehood: February 14, 1859

Origin of Name: Uncertain, but probably named for the Columbia River. The river was once called the Oregon, or Ouragan, French for "hurricane."

Nickname: The Beaver State

Capital: Salem

Motto: She Flies with Her Own Wings

Bird: Western meadowlark

Animal: Beaver

Flower: Oregon grape

Tree: Douglas fir

Insect: Oregon swallowtail butterfly

Nut: Hazelnut

Fish: Chinook salmon

Rock: Thunderegg

Gemstone: Sunstone

Colors: Navy blue and gold

Western meadowlark

Oregon swallowtail butterfly

OREGON, MY OREGON

Judge John A. Buchanan's poem "Oregon, My Oregon" was set to music by three different composers in a 1920 competition for official state song. This winning composition was adopted by the state legislature in 1927.

Words by John A. Buchanan   **Music by Henry B. Murtagh**

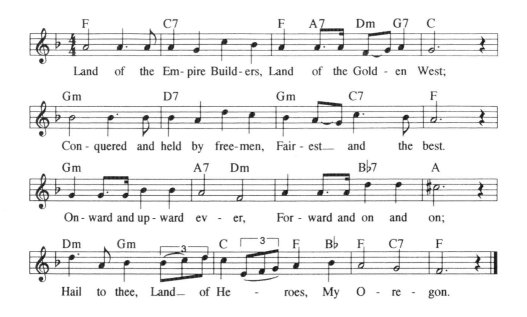

GEOGRAPHY

Highest Point: approximately 11,235 feet above sea level, at Mount Hood

Lowest Point: sea level, along the Pacific coast

Area: 98,386 square miles

Greatest Distance North to South: 295 miles

Greatest Distance East to West: 395 miles

Bordering States: Washington to the north, Idaho to the east, Nevada to the southeast and east, California to the south

Hottest Recorded Temperature: 119°F at Prineville on July 29, 1898, and at Pendleton on August 10, 1898

Coldest Recorded Temperature: −54°F at Ukiah on February 9, 1933, and at Seneca on February 10, 1933

Average Annual Precipitation: 28 inches

Major Rivers: Columbia, Deschutes, John Day, Owyhee, Rogue, Snake, Umpqua, Willamette

Major Lakes: Abert, Blue River, Bluejoint, Campbell, Chinook, Crane Prairie, Crater, Detroit, Fern Ridge, Flagstaff, Foster, Harney, Hart, Lookout Point, Malheur, Prineville, Summer, Upper Klamath, Waldo, Wallowa

Trees: alder, ash, cottonwood, Douglas fir, Engelmann spruce, juniper, lodgepole pine, madrone, maple, ponderosa pine, sugar pine, western hemlock, western red cedar, western white pine, willow

Wild Plants: buckbrush, bunch grass, camas lily, Indian paintbrush, juniper, Oregon grape, red huckleberry, sagebrush

Animals: antelope, beaver, bighorn sheep, bobcat, coyote, deer, elk, fox, mink, mountain goat, muskrat, river otter, sea lion, sea otter, seal, whale

Birds: bald eagle, duck, goose, grebe, grouse, hawk, heron, osprey, pelican, sandpiper, sora, spotted owl, swan, warbler, woodpecker

Fish: perch, salmon, steelhead trout, striped bass, sturgeon

Endangered Animals: black right whale, blue whale, fin whale, grey whale, grey wolf, humpback whale, sei whale, sperm whale

Endangered Plants: Applegates's milk vetch, big-flowered wooly meadow-foam, Bradshaw's desert-parsley, Cook's desert-parsley, crinite mariposa lily, Cusick's lupine, Dalles Mountain buttercup, Gentner's fritillary, golden paintbrush, Grimy ivesia, Howell's thelypody, MacFarlane's four o'clock, Malheur wire-lettuce, Mulford's milk vetch, northern wormwood, Owyhee clover, pink sand verbena, red-fruited lomatium, rough allocarya, saltmarsh bird's-beak, shiny-fruited allocarya, smooth mentzelia, Snake River goldenweed, Spalding's campion, Umpqua mariposa lily, western lily, white rock larkspur, Willamette daisy

Oregon grape

TIMELINE

Oregon History

c. 8000 B.C. Native Americans enter the region that will become Oregon.

1579 Sir Francis Drake may have landed on the Oregon coast.

1778 James Cook sails along the Oregon coast and names Cape Foulweather.

1792 Captain Robert Gray sails into the Columbia River and names it for his ship.

1805 Lewis and Clark reach the Pacific Ocean at the mouth of the Columbia River.

1811 John Jacob Astor founds Astoria as a fur-trading post.

1819 Spain surrenders its land claim north of 42° north latitude, establishing Oregon's straight southern border at this line.

1824 John McLoughlin, the "father of Oregon," becomes the director of the Hudson's Bay Company in Oregon.

1834 The first permanent settlement in the Willamette Valley is founded by missionaries.

1840s Settlers begin moving west on the Oregon Trail.

1848 Oregon becomes a territory.

1850 Congress passes the Oregon Donation Land Law, which gives land to settlers in the Oregon Territory.

1850 The territorial government is moved to Salem.

1851 Oregon's first public school opens.

1853 Congress creates Washington Territory, which establishes Oregon's present boundaries.

1859 Oregon becomes a state.

1872–1873 U.S. troops battle the Modoc Indians in the Modoc Wars.

1877 U.S. troops battle the Nez Percé in the Nez Percé War.

1912 Women are granted the right to vote in Oregon.

1937 The Bonneville Dam is completed, making the Columbia River navigable.

1940 The population of Oregon passes one million.

1950 Oregon becomes the nation's leading lumber state.

1964 Floods in western Oregon cause widespread damage.

1984 Oregon adopts a state lottery.

1980s The growth of high-technology industries creates an economic boom in the northern Willamette Valley, which earns the nickname Silicon Forest.

1990 Oregon voters pass Measure 5, limiting the taxes that owners must pay on their properties but creating budget problems for the state.

2005 Oregonians celebrate the two-hundredth anniversary of the Lewis and Clark expedition's visit to the Pacific Northwest.

ECONOMY

Agricultural Products: beans, beef cattle, berries, cherries, chickens, clover, corn, dairy cattle, flower bulbs, grass seed, hay, hazelnuts, hogs, hops, onions, pears, peas, plums, potatoes, sheep, sugar beets, timber (Douglas fir and ponderosa pine), wheat

Manufactured Products: computers, electrical equipment, frozen fruits and vegetables, lumber, machinery, paper, paperboard, particleboard, plywood, scientific instruments, veneer

Natural Resources: clays, copper, diatomite, gold, gravel, lead, limestone, natural gas, nickel, pumice, sand, silver chromium, soils, stone, timber, water

Anjou pears

Business and Trade: finance, insurance, international trade, printing and publishing, real estate, tourism

CALENDAR OF CELEBRATIONS

Portland Cinco de Mayo Cinco de Mayo is held on May 5 to celebrate the anniversary of Mexico's defeat of a French army in 1867. In Portland, the city's Mexican-American population hosts a huge, happy celebration that is one of the largest Hispanic celebrations in the Pacific Northwest.

Oregon Shakespeare Festival The plays of William Shakespeare and others come to life every year in Ashland from February through October.

Portland Rose Festival Oregon is famous for its flowers. The rose takes center stage every June in Portland. Carnivals, concerts, and other events add to the festive atmosphere, which is capped off by the Grand Floral Parade.

Cannon Beach Sand Castle Contest Contestants try to outdo each other by building the largest and fanciest sand castles they can each June. More than a hundred sand castles dot the beach until the tide washes them away.

Da Vinci Days Science and technology are celebrated at this unique science festival held every July in Corvallis. There are many displays and hands-on exhibits in this festival, which is named for Leonardo da Vinci.

July 4th Parade Each Independence Day, Hillsboro hosts the largest patriotic parade in the state.

World Championship Timber Carnival Oregon leads the country in timber production, and loggers and lumberjacks participate in such contests as log-rolling each Independence Day weekend in Albany.

Oregon Bach Festival Each summer, baroque music is celebrated through several performances at the beautiful Hult Center in Eugene.

Oregon Country Fair This summertime fair, held in July in Elmira, is the place to see some of the finest arts and crafts the state has to offer.

Oregon State Fair Horse races, a rodeo, and great food are some of the main attractions at "Oregon's biggest show," held each August in Salem.

Fall International Kite Festival The beautiful countryside around Lincoln City becomes even more colorful during this September celebration. Thousands of kites fill the sky.

Pendleton Round-Up and Happy Canyon Pageant Oregon's western heritage is celebrated during this rodeo. Musical shows and dances round out the September celebration.

Festival of Lights at the Grotto The holiday season is brightened each December with a beautiful display of Christmas lights in the trees at Portland's famous gardens.

Dick Fosbury (1947–) was born in Portland and attended Oregon State University. There he invented a new approach to the high jump. He flipped over the bar backward in a move that became known as the Fosbury Flop. He set an Olympic record in the 1968 summer Olympic Games in Mexico City. High jumpers around the world now use the jump Fosbury invented.

John E. Frohnmayer (1942–), who was appointed chairman of the National Endowment of the Arts in 1989, is a longtime supporter of the arts. Born in Medford, he has helped choose public artworks for the city of Eugene and for the Capitol in Salem. He served as chairman of the Oregon Arts Commission prior to 1989.

Matt Groening (1954–) is the creator of *The Simpsons* television show. Born in Portland, his love of cartooning started when he was in elementary school. The success of *The Simpsons* has led to the creation of more than 200 products. Despite his success, Groening says, "Most of all, I'm in this business to have fun."

Mark Odom Hatfield (1922–) served in the U.S. Senate from 1966 to 1997. He was born in Dallas, Oregon, and was elected to the state legislature in 1950. He served as a representative for four years and then as a state senator for two more years. After serving as Oregon's secretary of state, he was elected governor in 1959.

Donald P. Hodel (1935–) was born in Portland. He served as the secretary of energy and later as the secretary of the interior under President Reagan. He sparked controversy because he favored opening public lands to oil companies and supported the development of nuclear power.

Matt Groening

Dave Kingman (1948–) is a heavy-hitting baseball player known as Dave "Kong" Kingman. Born in Pendleton, he broke Little League records as a young ballplayer. This right-hander, a reliable long-distance hitter (he has several three-homer games to his credit), has played for many teams.

Ursula K. Le Guin (1929–) is among the greatest science-fiction and fantasy writers and one of Portland's leading residents. She began writing at age nine. Her novels address many issues in fantastic settings.

Edwin Markham (1852–1940), a great poet, was born in a log cabin in Oregon City. From these simple beginnings, he rose to become the "Dean of American Poetry." Markham's most famous works are "The Man with the Hoe" and "Lincoln, Man of the People." Today, 150 years after his birth, his poems are still widely read and admired.

Tom McCall (1913–1983) grew up on the family ranch near Prineville. As a boy he loved Oregon's great outdoors. As governor from 1967 to 1975, he fought hard to preserve Oregon's natural beauty and resources.

Joaquin Miller (1837–1913) traveled from Indiana to Oregon as a boy. He became a showman and poet, relating exciting tales about life in Oregon and other parts of the American West. His autobiography tells the tale of his life among the Modoc Indians.

Linus Pauling (1901–1994) was born in Portland. A brilliant chemist, he received the Nobel Prize in Chemistry in 1954. Pauling worked to ban nuclear weapons tests. He spearheaded an antitesting petition, which more than 11,000 scientists from around the world signed. The petition urged the United Nations to work to stop nuclear testing and helped lead to the Nuclear Test Ban Treaty in 1963. Pauling was awarded the Nobel Peace Prize in 1962. Pauling also championed the use of vitamin C as an important part of a healthy diet.

Linus Pauling

John Reed (1887–1920) was born into a wealthy Oregon family in Portland. As a young journalist, he covered the Mexican Revolution and World War I. As his interest in social problems grew, he moved to Russia and became a supporter of the Bolsheviks. He died in Russia and was buried in the Kremlin. His book *Ten Days That Shook the World* is an eyewitness account of the Russian Revolution.

Alberto Salazar (1958–   ) is one of the greatest long-distance runners of all time. As a student at the University of Oregon, he qualified for the U.S. Olympic team. Salazar won the New York Marathon three years in a row and was also victorious in the Boston Marathon.

William Stafford (1914–1993) was a leading American poet. He won the prestigious National Book Award in 1963 for his book of verse *Traveling through the Dark*. In 1975 he was named the Poet Laureate of Oregon, a post he held until his death.

TOUR THE STATE

Dee Wright Observatory (Sisters) This is the site of Oregon's largest lava flow. A trail lets visitors explore the bizarre landscape where astronauts trained before heading to the moon.

Newberry National Volcanic Monument (LaPine) The world's largest obsidian flow, odd lava formations, and beautiful waterfalls and lakes are discussed by National Forest Service naturalists, who conduct walking tours of this one-of-a-kind place.

Smith Rock State Park (Redmond) One of the most beautiful places in a beautiful state, this park offers stunning views of spectacular rock formations.

Malheur National Wildlife Refuge (Burns) More than 250 species of birds, including trumpeter swans, thrive in this refuge. Many mammals, such as antelope and mink, can also be seen here.

Hells Canyon National Recreation Area (Joseph) At the overlook, visitors stand more than a mile above the floor of the deepest gorge in North America.

National Historic Oregon Trail Interpretive Center (Baker City) Visitors learn about the hardships and joys of life on the Oregon Trail through the many exhibits and reenactments here.

John Day Fossil Beds National Monument (John Day) More than 50 million years of the earth's history are visible in this rich landscape. Saber-toothed tigers and giant pigs once roamed here, and their fossils are on display.

Collier State Park (Klamath Falls) Explore Oregon's most important industry at the largest logging museum in the United States. Exhibits teach about the history and workings of the timber industry.

Crater Lake National Park Crater Lake is the deepest lake in the country and one of the most beautiful sites in the world. National park rangers explain the origin of the lake and point out the many plants and animals that thrive here.

Fort Clatsop National Memorial (Fort Clatsop) The fort Lewis and Clark built to survive the winter of 1805–1806 has been re-created. Guides discuss the fort and the many artifacts on display.

Oregon Coast Aquarium (Newport) A large shark habitat is a major attraction of this huge aquarium. Many other types of marine and coastal life can also be viewed here.

Oregon Coast Aquarium

Oregon Dunes National Recreation Center (Florence) This "natural sandbox" is 40 miles long! Oregonians and tourists hike and camp along these beautiful sandy beaches year-round.

The Capitol (Salem) Daily tours teach about the history of Oregon and its beautiful capitol building.

Gilbert House Children's Museum (Salem) This fun museum for children offers dozens of hands-on displays in fourteen activity rooms. The museum focuses on arts, humanities, and the sciences. Activities range from making puppets to operating a model hydroelectric dam.

Corvallis Arts Center (Corvallis) Housed in a 100-year-old church, artworks are displayed year-round.

Portland Art Museum (Portland) The feature attraction of this museum is its Northwest Coast Indian collection, which is one of the most impressive of its kind.

The Willamette Science and Technology Center (Eugene) Young people of Eugene and visitors from all over participate in hands-on science and technology experiments and activities at WISTEC.

University of Oregon Museum of Art (Eugene) This museum houses the Warner Collection of Oriental Art, which is among the best-known collections of Asian artwork in the United States.

Oregon Museum of Science and Industry (Portland) A submarine and a planetarium are just two of the fascinating exhibits at the premier education facility in the Northwest.

Oregon Zoo (Portland) Instead of living in cages, the animals in this zoo thrive in specially constructed natural habitats.

The Columbia River Gorge National Scenic Area The Columbia River Gorge is celebrated for its stunning natural beauty. Enjoy the view by hiking and camping along its banks or travel through the gorge in a tour boat.

Bonneville Dam (Bonneville) This huge dam provides electric power and flood control along the Columbia River. Special "fish ladders" let salmon swimming upstream leap past the dam.

Mount Hood At approximately 11,235 feet, this beautiful landmark is the highest mountain in the state. Dozens of campgrounds, hiking trails, and parks in the region offer breathtaking views of Mount Hood.

FUN FACTS

Portland is home to the world's smallest official park. Measuring just two feet across, Mill Ends Park was established as an official city park in 1976. It was created in 1948 as a home for leprechauns and a place to hold snail races on St. Patrick's Day.

The world's largest cheese factory, the Tillamook Cheese Factory, is located in Oregon.

Find Out More

If you'd like to find out more about Oregon, look in your school library, local library, bookstore, or video and DVD store. Here are some titles to start with:

GENERAL STATE BOOKS

Bratvold, Gretchen. *Oregon,* 2nd edition. Minneapolis: Lerner, 2003.

Ingram, Scott W. *Oregon* (America the Beautiful, Second Series). Danbury, CT: Children's Press, 2000.

Noblie, Iris. *Oregon.* New York: Coward-McCann, 1996.

Shannon, Terry Miller. *Oregon* (From Sea to Shining Sea, Second Series). Danbury, CT: Children's Press, 2003.

BOOKS ABOUT OREGON PEOPLE, PLACES, OR HISTORY

Isaacs, Sally S. *The Oregon Trail.* Chicago: Heinemann Library, 2004.

Official Oregon Kid's Guide. Salem: Oregon Tourism Commission, 2004.

Smolan, Rick and Davic D. Elliott, editors. *Oregon 24/7.* New York: DK, 2004.

CD-ROMS

The Oregon Trail, 5th edition. The Learning Company, 2004.

DVDS AND VIDEOS

Lewis and Clark: Great Journey West. National Geographic Society, 2002.

Oregon, State of Wonder. Mellnik, 2001.

The Oregon Trail. Educational Video Network, 2001.

WEB SITES

The Oregon Blue Book

www.bluebook.state.or.us.

This is the state's official directory and fact book site containing information about government operations and agencies, as well as facts useful to students and teachers. Separate sections cover such topics as a detailed history, an economic overview, information about the state's Indian tribes and reservations, facts about the Lewis and Clark expedition, and biographies of notable Oregonians.

The Oregon Historical Society

www.ohs.org

This Web site has many online resources. The history of Oregon emphasizes the roles and contributions of the state's various ethnic groups. There are also many historical documents, photos, and video documentaries.

The Multnomah County Library

www.multcolib.org/homework/natamhc.html

This Web site for students contains information about Oregon's Native Americans. It provides links to dozens of librarian-reviewed Web sites on Native American history and culture in Oregon, the Pacific Northwest, and beyond.

Index

Page numbers in **boldface** are illustrations and charts.

ABOUT THE AUTHOR

Rebecca Stefoff is the author of numerous books for young readers. Many of her books are about American history. She has written about Oregon and the Oregon Trail in *The Opening of the West* (Benchmark, 2003), Stefoff lives in Portland, Oregon. You can learn more about her and her books at her Web site, www.rebeccastefoff.com.